CONFLICT

HANDLING CONFLICT
IN THE LOCAL CHURCH

PAULINE BELL & PAULINE JORDAN

Scripture Union
130 City Road London EC1V 2NJ

© Pauline Bell and Pauline Jordan 1992

First published 1992

ISBN 0 86201 774 2

Scripture quotations in this publication are from the Holy Bible, New International Version. Copyright © 1973, 1978, 1984 International Bible Society. Published by Hodder and Stoughton.

The right of Pauline Bell and Pauline Jordan to be identi-fied as authors of this work has been asserted by them in accordance with the Copyright, Designs and Patents Act 1988.

British Library Cataloguing-in-Publication Data.
A catalogue record for this book is available from the British Library.

Cover and book design by Julian Smith.

Phototypeset by Intype, London.

Printed and bound in Great Britain by Cox and Wyman Ltd, Reading.

Contents

Acknowledgements

This book would never have been written without the dynamic of our friendship. We would each want to acknowledge with gratitude the contribution of the other; any differences we had proved wholly constructive in sharpening what eventually went on the page.

We wish to thank the Training Unit of Scripture Union, with whom we both work, who gave vital personal support to Pauline Bell during a very painful local church conflict; and we thank also the group of local Christians who engaged with us in a lengthy process of trying to make sense of that experience.

We are deeply grateful to the Revd Juliet Montague, one time chaplain at Lincoln Cathedral, now minister in charge of the parishes of Whaplode Drove and Gedney Hill, Lincolnshire, whose counselling skill enabled both of us in very different ways to work out the emotions that conflict gives rise to, so that the process of redemption could begin. Juliet, along with Joan King of the Scripture Union Training

Unit, kindly read the first draft and they both made some invaluable suggestions.

September 1991

Introduction

We would like to have called this book *Jesus wept*, an emotive title which came to us almost accidentally. We both belong to a small group of Christians who have two things in common: our faith and our painful experiences of the local church. What has happened to us has led all but two of us to leave one local church and not feel able to face getting really involved in another. One evening as we shared our progress with this book we started to brainstorm ideas for a title and somehow *Jesus wept* floated to the surface.

At first, we rejected this because, though not trained theologians, we respect the scriptures sufficiently not to want to wrest things out of context. However, the more we thought about it the more it seemed to feel right. There are two occasions when Jesus is recorded as weeping: one is in the context of his grief at the death of Lazarus, and the other over the city of Jerusalem which was in subsequent days to witness the cosmic conflict of the cross. On both occasions Jesus was grieving because of loss: the loss of a life and a friend, for the lost state of humankind and, particularly in Jerusalem, for people who were closed and not listening. Many of these people were leaders and, as the conflict unfolds, we witness them so often betraying their positions of trust, particularly when we read that 'all the people kept listening to him, not wanting to miss a single word'. Nevertheless, it is important to recognise that some of the leaders, like Joseph and Nicodemus, did listen, and some of the people crying 'Crucify!' to Pilate were ordinary people. It is vital not to label groups as 'goodies and baddies' like the cowboys and Indians in the story line of old films.

We do not believe that all conflict is unhelpful; in fact, it can be tremendously creative and give new life through its stimulating effect. Diversity and difference are aspects of creation and life to be both acknowledged and valued. God made the world full of tension, counter-tension and paradox; everything is complex. Yet we live in a world which is imperfect and fallen, and so often things which are good in themselves become destructive rather than creative. This was our experience of conflict in the local church. We felt deeply and we grieved over the loss of trust and friendship. We felt betrayed, frequently misunderstood and rarely listened to. No doubt others on the other side of the chasm of conflict felt likewise. We believe it is in such situations that Jesus weeps – but, thankfully, he also redeems, and we hope that this book will be part of the redemption of our experiences.

We are both trainers committed to working at

our own growth and development; we also offer our skills to enable others to grow. This often involves helping people to learn from their experiences of life, as well as from experiences that we plan as part of a training event. We sometimes find that during such an event things happen that we have not planned at all, and part of our skill is to respond to the dynamic which has arisen unexpectedly in order to help people learn from it. Usually some conflict is involved. The jargon word for such happenings in any kind of group is the 'process'.

Jesus often worked with the process of a group, as on the occasion when he was speaking to his disciples about his coming death: 'the Son of Man is going to be betrayed into the hands of men' (Luke 9:44). The course of his teaching is interrupted by a spontaneous argument among the disciples as to which of them would be the greatest (Luke 9:46). Jesus is quite prepared to break off to deal with the 'here and now', that is, the process of what was happening in the group. He addressed the issue immediately, using a nearby child as an example: 'whoever welcomes this little child in my name welcomes me; and whoever welcomes me welcomes the one who sent me. For he who is least among you all – he is the greatest' (Luke 9:48). The disciples' learning was, therefore, earthed in their shared life experience, often arising unexpectedly from the incidents of daily living: it was not solely the result of Jesus' prepared teaching programme. How often do we in our church groups stop the agenda, whether it is the teaching programme or

11

the business meeting, to deal with people's reactions, feelings and behaviour in the 'here and now'? All our interactions, one to one, in groups or on committees, have the potential for learning.

Many life experiences are deeply painful, and we believe that many people, whether they are conscious of it or not, reflect on such experiences in order to make sense of them. Our small group came together initially for mutual support and to try to understand what had happened to us. It did not prove easy and some of us are still struggling, whilst others are beginning to know a redemption from pain. For me (Pauline Bell), the acceptance offered by the group and the constant support of my work colleagues, as well as individual counselling, enabled me to believe in God's acceptance of me when those whom I had counted as my friends in the local church were suggesting my faith was lacking and rejecting me by refusing to receive me in my emotional vulnerability. The more I reflect on this, the more I realise that whether in leadership or not they were unable to do so because they too are fallen; they too were damaged from past experiences and, like me, lacked the skills or the emotional energy to analyse what was happening at the time. They were therefore unable to respond creatively.

This book, therefore, is an attempt on our part to write down what we have learned from experience of conflict in the local church. There is still much to learn. Integrated into our working practice as trainers and into the way we handle life is a model known as

Kolb's[1] learning cycle:

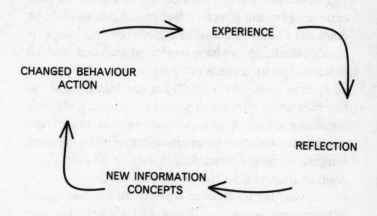

In this book we share incidents and case studies that come out of the experiences of ourselves and of others. Obviously we have had to distort specific details to protect the innocent and guilty alike, always supposing that we can tell which is which. Perhaps all parties are both. The events in these studies are looked at from different angles and using different lenses, reminiscent of the story about looking at the dome of St Paul's Cathedral: from below it is concave, from above it is convex. Yet it is the same building, the only difference being the viewpoint. When exploring conflict there are usually more than two aspects to a situation, and the journey of reflection is complex.

From this process of reflection we have begun to add to our knowledge and understanding of conflict.

We have both had training in conflict management, and have read about and around the topic. We may offer insights and pointers, but would not want to be definitive. Making sense of experience has taken us back to the Bible; we have conferred with and listened to what is written there as a part of the whole process of making sense of events. What has happened to us, together with the reasons we have for feeling that this book might be helpful to others, has led us to focus on conflict which is destructive rather than creative. For this reason a great deal more can be said about conflict than will be found in these pages.

As well as case studies, we have used prose, story-telling, activities and dialogue to facilitate our own thought-processes as well as that of our readers. We believe that readers will bring knowledge and understanding to this subject far beyond any tentative conclusions we may offer.

In conclusion, what we are trying to achieve is:

■ to share our experiences of conflict in the local church
■ to explore the processes and factors that may be found in conflict situations
■ to consider possible ways of handling conflict when it arises
■ to identify different practices that might prevent unhelpful conflict surfacing in the first place

To fulfil these objectives, the book is structured in the following way:

Chapters one to six explore the factors that surround conflict situations and, particularly in the dialogues, offer possible ways of handling conflict as the beginnings of polarisation are recognised in a group.

Chapter seven looks at conflict situations in the Bible in the light of the previous chapters.

Chapter eight focuses on change, which is almost always the catalyst for the beginning of conflict. We therefore look at ways of handling change. Chapters nine and ten focus on things that need attention if unnecessary conflict is to be avoided.

Chapter eleven, on mediation, shows how a way may be found through conflicts which have resulted in the breakdown of communication and relationships. It is intended only as a demonstration of a possible way of working, and is not intended in any way to be a 'How To' guide.

REFERENCES

1 Kolb D A & Fry R, 'Towards an Applied Theory of Experiential Learning' in *Theories of Group Processes*, Cooper C L (ed), John Wiley & Sons, London, 1975.

CHAPTER 1

A CASE OF CONFLICT

Colin was already a lay reader and a committed member of the Anglican church when the new vicar came. He had had a close friendship with the previous vicar who had seen him as a gifted preacher and an excellent colleague. The father of two sons, Colin was separated from his wife. No third person was involved in their split and they remained on good terms. Colin and Hilary had tried for many years to save their marriage but finally, after many discussions with a counsellor and a great deal of prayer, they all felt that separation was the best course of action in the circumstances. They had talked with the children, who as teenagers were now old enough to understand something of the situation and the implications. They also discussed it with the vicar who was very support-ive. Colin's wife found a job in a town about fifty miles away and the boys remained with Colin so that they need not change schools.

As the licensed lay reader, Colin was soon noticed by the new incumbent, and it was entirely natural that he should become a member of the leadership team set up by Tom, the vicar, a year after his arrival in the parish.

At first, all went well. Tom's vision of shared leadership and every-member ministry was being realised through the involvement of people like Colin and others who undertook a variety of tasks. But time passed by and Tom began to realise that he was not entirely comfortable having Colin on the team. There were times when he found Colin's marriage situation difficult, and it was then that Tom became aware of a background of criticism towards Colin's broken marriage among certain members of the congregation.

Tom met with Colin and told him that he was removing him from the leadership team. The reason he gave was that Colin could not be allowed to engage in any preaching because he was in a state of sin. Since marriage vows are for life and divorce is sinful in the sight of God, separation is a sin and Colin's situation made him spiritually vulnerable and unfit to be in leadership. Further, Colin's presence would weaken the work of the leadership team. He quoted 1 Timothy 3:12 – 'A deacon must be the husband of but one wife and must manage his children and his household well'.

Colin was devastated and stunned into silence by the unexpectedness of it all. Once the news was out, some of Colin's leadership team colleagues became extremely angry about the way he had been treated; they even voiced their anger to Tom, who was adamant that Colin must go.

The leadership team met without Colin or Tom to discuss the whole issue. Amid the anger, confusion and feelings of injustice in the group grew criticism of Tom over what was seen as pastoral ineptness. When they later met with Tom, they told him that they felt that the way he had handled the situation amounted to mismanagement bordering on incompetence. They were also unhappy that, having been committed to shared leadership, Tom had on this occasion acted unilaterally.

Tom was now standing alone. His immediate response was to cancel leadership team meetings and to withdraw from contact with members of the church. The anger and frustration resulting from this plunged the church into disarray and led inevitably to confrontation between those who thought Colin had been treated unjustly and the minority who had been critical of Colin because of his broken marriage. Tom's attitude was: I am in authority; it is your responsibility to submit to my leadership. He called for repentance on the part of those who had disagreed with him.

Colin and two other members of the leadership team eventually left the church. The team never met again and in fact four years later none of the members had ever taken part in any kind of leadership. No similar team was re-formed by Tom, who after three years left the church.

What is your view?

■ Try to identify with Tom. Explore all the possibilities:

    (i) what prompted his action in relation to Colin?

    (ii) what caused his subsequent actions?

■ Explore the thoughts and feelings of Colin and of his friends:

    (i) when Tom first removed him from leadership;

    (ii) when he began to think things through;

    (iii) when he realised others on the leadership team were also angry;

    (iv) after three months when Tom was demanding submission and not willing to discuss issues openly.

■ How do you think the events outlined would affect:

    (i) the members of the leadership team?

    (ii) the church as a whole?

(No character details are given, so respond to this as if you were one of the team who had a good working relationship with both Colin and Tom up until the incident.)

The case study outlined above is based on four separate incidents in four different congregations, all of different denominations. It is, for the purposes of discussion, deliberately written to make the issues fairly clear cut. Rarely in conflict situations are things quite like that, though it might happen.

What are the factors contributing to this particular conflict which might, to a greater or lesser degree, contribute to major or even minor conflicts within any local church?

Tom brought to his post a particular theology of leadership and the laity. For this reason he organised the church with a leadership team made up entirely of lay people. One of the many consequences of such a model is that, theoretically, it removes power from the minister by sharing it among members of a team. But how far had Tom faced that and thought it through?

In addition, Tom's theology of marriage was clearly defined. The fact that Colin was already an accepted lay reader placed Tom in an immediate dilemma. Did he recognise this dilemma? Is it possible that he was paralysed by the status quo and failed to identify tensions within himself about Colin's marital status at the time? Was the desire to fulfil his vision for shared leadership prompting him to press ahead too rapidly?

Perhaps, as he began to work with Colin, there were things about him that Tom found difficult, so he did not relate comfortably to him as a person. How might Tom have perceived Colin's gifts and skills? He may have begun, consciously or sub-consciously, to give greater significance to Colin's marital status as a way of rationalising, with the support of the Bible, a growing conviction that Colin should be removed from the team. The criticism of Colin from others in the congregation may have been seen as a threat to his own ministry. Certainly lack of confidence in the leadership team would be unhelpful to his own position. He may have felt, quite genuinely, that he needed to repent of inviting Colin onto the team, which he now saw as a mistake.

Tom's actions from this point bear all the marks of someone out of his depth. Having put a match to the touch paper, he loses control of the subsequent fire.

Lack of communication becomes the predominant feature of the ensuing conflict. Tom's original doubts about Colin do not seem to have been explored either with Colin or with anyone else; hence, Colin's removal is a shock for all the leadership team. Tom's eventual cancellation of meetings and his withdrawal suggest that his emotions are very complex at this time. His behaviour may have been prompted by fear of not being able to handle the people involved in face-to-face meetings, in which case he would have felt isolated and alone. A turbulence of emotion bordering on panic might be paralysing him.

Meanwhile, Colin and his friends were in a state of shock. Colin in particular felt it to be a final and cruel blow, coming as it did at the end of two years in which he and Hilary had weathered a painful decision to separate, and Colin, with their two sons, had had to make considerable adjustments in their new life together. With support from some, though not all, in the church they had survived the worst of it, and Colin had entered with enthusiasm into Tom's vision for shared leadership.

Tom's rejection of him as a member of the leadership team, and the stated reasons for it, came as an emotional body blow. Colin had coped with his work and the needs of his sons all through the separation, but the suddenness and shock of this event took him to breaking point: he found deep emotions surfacing and became panic-stricken that he would break down in public as he could not cope with expressions of sympathy. He did not know whether he felt hurt, angry or bewildered, but he knew it was complex and painful. As a Christian he felt he should 'turn the other cheek', but the reality was that he felt more like hitting someone, preferably Tom.

Three months later, Tom was still inflexible. He was by now demanding that the others on the leadership team who had supported Colin should repent of this and submit to his leadership.

Colin began to feel totally powerless. He and Tom seemed to be working from different value systems, yet both believed that they were living by scripture. It felt as if there were no way across the chasm which had opened up between them. Even a starting point was impossible with Colin wanting to engage in discussion, adult-to-adult, and Tom declaring he was God's appointed leader and that Colin must submit to him. Colin realised he was facing a second separation, though he still believed that reconciliation with Tom ought to be possible.

The rest of the leadership team were also experiencing turbulent emotion as they grappled to make sense of what had happened. They felt they had been made powerless by Tom's action, and in particular they thought he had betrayed his commitment to shared leadership. Bewilderment, confusion, insecurity, uncertainty and anger were everywhere.

Other members of the church were equally bewildered. Some felt that it had been a mistake for Colin to be in leadership, while others mistrusted the existence of such a team anyway. Many felt sad for Colin and believed he had been treated unfairly. There was much confusion over Tom's reason for his actions. For a while, it became the main topic of conversation, but this simply added to the pain. An opinion was expressed that Colin had been made a scapegoat. When Colin left the church, other members of the team left with him and some members of the church followed. There was a general loss of confidence in Tom. Sadly, Colin and some of the others were for some time unable to face joining another congregation.

The above case history and commentary may seem extreme. It reflects a side of church life which we as church members prefer to believe does not exist, and indeed would never happen in our own community. Yet these things do happen and we need to face this fact.

In subsequent chapters we shall explore in more detail the causes of conflict in the local church. We shall look at how to prevent conflict, but realistically we shall also discuss how to deal with it openly if it does occur. No matter what the nature of the conflict is – whether it be a conflict of needs, theology, leadership/followership styles, emotions, values, or a complex mixture of any or all of these – it is important to recognise that powerful emotions will always be present. We sometimes fail to recognise in a conflict situation that feelings are an important factor, and that such feelings need to be recognised and handled. It is unhelpful in attempts to resolve the situation to ignore another's anger or hurt because, whether we perceive these emotions as justified or not, they are very real for the person feeling them and they strongly influence all communication.

We both have very strong views and feelings about the kind of issues raised by the case study outlined above, as well as case studies in subsequent chapters. At times, these views and feelings will be obvious; they derive from our needs, emotions, values, style and theology, and we acknowledge that it is not possible, or even desirable, for us to be completely objective. Much better that we are aware of our own views and feelings, and that we own up to them. Then we are able to dialogue with others who have a different perspective. Moreover, whilst challenging things we see in local churches and thus revealing something of our own stance, we want to avoid suggesting 'this is right' and 'this is wrong', particularly in the case studies. If anything, we both believe that, like truth, such situations are rarely plain and never simple. Our intention is rather to invite our readers, through the text and the exercises, to use their own minds and form their own opinions.

CHAPTER 2

CONFLICTING NEEDS

Conflict in churches comes in many and varied guises: however, it is the ineffective management of it, rather than its mere presence, that leads to disaster.

Any committee or organisation requires a certain amount of conflict in order to grow and develop. Without it, individuals become set in their ways; they fail to examine ways of doing things and lose sight of their goals. In this situation the community becomes ineffective. Conflict also alleviates boredom: it kindles interest and encourages creative innovation.

Yet the very word 'conflict' raises disquiet in the hearts of most people. The history of the church is a catalogue of many unresolved conflicts: all too often the result was that people went their separate ways as individuals or groups. It is important to acknowledge that some conflicts may reach a point where separation is the most creative option, given human nature and the varying capacities of individuals to cope with the inevitable stress caused by conflict.

There are those, and we would be amongst them,

who would argue that going separate ways should be the last resort, to be used only if other means of resolving the conflict cannot be found. We as human beings would have to be fully secure and mature if conflict were always to be resolved without separation.

Most of us become vulnerable for many reasons. It may be the result of past interpersonal relationship problems, especially those between parents and growing children; or it may be because of the less than perfect nature of wider society, such as the vulnerability many women feel in a patriarchal society; or it may be because of personal sin. To expect resolution in every conflict situation is to presuppose a state of perfection.

Adding to the complexity is the fact that all too often the apparent problem seen as the main source of conflict is, in reality, masking several different problems. The individuals caught up in a conflict always have needs that will be either met by the change or threatened by it. For example, if I live alone and have made close friends in my home group whose fortnightly meetings are a focal point for that network of relationships, a proposal to rearrange home groups may feel like the equivalent of telling families that they have to pool and re-assign their children. The deep friendships formed in my particular group fulfil my desire for love, acceptance, support and belonging. Change could be quite traumatic and could lead to deprivation. Whenever needs are not met, deprivation will be the outcome. Having said that, it is important not to confuse the term 'need' with 'want'. For example, we all occasionally need a break from work; we may prefer the break to take the form of a holiday abroad, but that is a 'want', not a 'need'.

Let us look at the needs of Colin, from the case study in chapter one. After the separation from his wife, he needed acceptance, love and status in the sense of a recognised place where he could use his gifts to serve the church community. At first he needed practical and emotional support from church friends as he and his sons adjusted to a new home situation. He would then continue to need the emotional support of other adults with whom he could share his concerns; he needed people in his life whom he could trust and who were committed to him.

At the same time, Tom's needs were to fulfil his vision of shared leadership and every member ministry; he needed to find a way of living out these values, derived as he saw it from scripture. Above all he needed Colin on the leadership team, otherwise a man seen by others in the church as a leader could become a rallying point in a situation of dissent or disaffection. Colin's support, therefore, had to be openly expressed. But Tom's need for personal security made it difficult for him to work in any situation that was not clear-cut, not black or white. Colin's marital problems broke Tom's own rules and, as he perceived it, God's rules. Colin's situation made Tom feel insecure and uncertain, weakening his sense of being in the right place before God which was the mainspring of his authority. As a result, Tom felt spiritually vulnerable because he believed Colin did not qualify for biblical leadership as defined in Paul's epistles. At its most simple, Tom's sense of security was threatened by Colin's presence on the leadership team.

It is important to avoid making judgments when looking at a conflict issue; more important is to recognise the different needs surfacing there. Colin needed love, acceptance and a place to serve: his very presence threatened Tom who needed those sharing his leadership to be beyond reproach.

Most leaders need success. If there is little or no evidence of fulfilment of vision, or of God's blessing on his work, then a leader will look for a reason why. Then it is all too easy, particularly if some in the congregation are critical of the leadership, to look for a scapegoat. The victim will often be the most vulnerable, in this case Colin. Making somebody a scapegoat is often one of the ways in which leaders and church congregation cope with what Jung called 'the repressed shadow', where people close their minds to things inside themselves which they find too disturbing to acknowledge. However, when those things are seen mirrored in others, there may be a strong emotional response; for example, a person with an insecure marriage could be very negative towards someone who is divorced. Tom saw Colin as spiritually vulnerable and he felt this might affect the whole team and its work. Furthermore, as vicar, Tom would be watched, as would those he had chosen to share leadership. They must all have credibility in practising what they preached. For his own sake, Tom needed that credibility and needed to be seen to have authority as he preached on moral and theological issues or when he gave advice on the problems of life.

The issue, therefore, is not who was right in this conflict; the focus instead should be on the different needs around and the way those needs impinged on the situation. Admittedly, needs are not the only factor, but they make a significant contribution to any conflict scenario.

To take what seems at first a relatively insignificant example:

Ada Balin, now aged 70, had always made and served the tea when her church served light refreshments to the public. One Bank Holiday afternoon, the new steward, Jim, who was organising the day and was unaware of Ada's role, asked another person much younger than Ada to do it. When Ada found she had been replaced, she grumbled and soon found allies among her own age group. When this was related to Jim he expressed the opinion that Ada was too old to be handling a heavy tea pot and ignored the undercurrents of discontent. His own over-riding concern was to find enough reliable helpers to ensure that the day would be run with efficiency and style. However, Ada's former monopoly of the tea-making had given her a sense of place and of value. To be made redundant, as she saw it, left her feeling devalued.

31

The Bank Holiday event was Jim's first venture as a newly appointed steward. He found it difficult to sort out all the jobs and to know on whom to call. His insecurity made him anxious to succeed and he needed a boost for his self-esteem and confidence. Having failed to ask Ada, he did not then have the skills to sort out the ensuing conflict. He baulked at having to explain the situation to Pat, who had already agreed to do the job, and at having to apologise to Ada in an attempt to resolve the situation. Instead he chose to view Ada as an intransigent old woman, resistant to change, and rationalised it to himself and to others in terms of the risk to someone of her age from heavy apparatus and scalding water – but he did not speak to her.

Thus the conflict rumbled on with the result that neither Ada nor Jim had any respect for each other. An unhealthy festering of discontent became a permanent feature of their relationship. Ada's friends joined in her condemnation of Jim. In his defence, it should be noted that this whole situation might have been avoided if Jim's predecessor had briefed him properly, or had left written records concerning the organisation of church events.

This saga should not be seen as insignificant since to view it as such would be to devalue the people concerned. Jesus offered to those around him respect and care, whoever they were. If God sets a high value on individuals and their concerns, we must do the same to avoid unnecessary hurt. We need to ensure that people like Jim receive helpful preparation and training for their tasks and appropriate support when they embark on them. They need to feel such support, yet also to have the freedom to experiment as they take on an increasing amount of responsibility. How many people given responsibilities like Jim's in a church are also given a regular time with someone in leadership to discuss their work and their feelings about it? This kind of supportive supervision could be very helpful in averting mistakes or learning from them, thus preventing unnecessary damage.

The point being made here is that however altruistic or pure in heart we may hope we are, our own needs in such contexts will consciously – or sometimes unconsciously – affect our opinions. There is often a hidden agenda.

In the following example, the arguments have deliberately been presented as more simplistic than would probably be the case in real life.

Rev Keith Times – minister, in post for about two years, his first post 'in charge'.
Nancy Smith – President of the local WI, very involved in village matters, with a real concern for the elderly.
Peter Square – new to the village, lives on the executive estate, leads a busy life and has a high income.
Sarah Keel – long-standing member of the church, getting on in years, pensioner, not well-off.
Chris Keeper – youth leader, with a fairly passionate concern for social issues.

The people above comprise a sub-committee concerned with the allocation of Harvest gifts. Traditionally, these were given to local elderly people but recently they have been auctioned off and the proceeds used to buy Christmas hampers for them instead.

THE MEETING

Keith opened with prayer, thanking God for his faithfulness in providing £727 from the Harvest Auction collection. He also prayed that God's will would be done concerning how the money would be distributed.

Chris proposed that the money should be given to Help the Aged for the use of elderly people in poorer countries. (Chris has done voluntary work with Christian Aid and sees the Third World as more worthy of concern than his own village. He has been involved with a project for the elderly.)

Peter supported Chris's idea. He stated his belief that elderly people in the Third World are much worse off than anyone in the village. (Peter has a conscience that nags occasionally about giving to such charities as OXFAM. He sees a chance to salve his conscience. He was among those who bid high for such items as bunches of beetroot.)

Sarah reminded the meeting of village people who relied on getting the hampers in time for Christmas. (Sarah would be one of the recipients and would really miss this contribution at such an expensive time of the year.)

Nancy agreed with Sarah as she knows many elderly people have only their state pension and would depend on the Christmas hamper. (Nancy was voted into office as President by many of the elderly people of the village. She would not want them to know that she had spoken in favour of these gifts going elsewhere.)

Keith commented on the difficulty facing them. Both their own elderly and those in the Third World deserved their support. (Keith does not know how to cope with such opposing views and yet sees the merits of both. He does not want to risk the displeasure of either side.)

To Think Through

■ With which of these characters do you most identify? What were the reasons for your choice?

■ When the different opinions had been expressed, what do you think the character you have identified with would want from the meeting?

■ Still thinking of that individual, what needs might that be meeting in him or her?

■ If you haven't thought about Keith, what do you think he could do in this situation?

■ Focus on an issue that has recently been discussed (preferably heatedly) in a group of which you are a part. If it was a change you

---

> resisted, can you identify specific ways in
> which you felt threatened? In other words,
> what needs met by the status quo did the
> proposed change threaten? If you were in
> favour, what needs will be, or might have
> been, met for you?

Keith's concern is probably different from the others'. As chairperson he has to handle the conflict. Although anyone on the committee could take the initiative to resolve the conflict, it is likely that Keith will be left to do so as the minister, the chairperson and the one with most to gain by resolving the situation to everyone's satisfaction.

Most of the arguments openly expressed are in themselves reasonable, but each person has a hidden motive.

Chris has had first-hand experience of something he is enthusiastic about and which colours his thinking in relation to any money to be given away. He is driven by the need to do something about a situation that concerns and enthuses him.

Peter knows that much of his high income goes to pay the mortgage. He feels guilty about his lack of giving in the face of Third World poverty and, having made a significant contribution to the Harvest auction, his need to salve his conscience could be met by seeing his money go to the Third World.

Sarah has real financial needs and she depends upon the gift at Christmas. She feels panic at the thought that it might not happen this year.

Nancy has missed out on a career and the WI role meets her need for status in the local community. Through it, she has an outlet for her organisational skills. Not being President would be like being made redundant.

Keith dislikes contention and having to handle it. He needs to feel accepted and liked in the village and finds the insecurity of unpopularity difficult to bear.

It is very easy to look at a situation like this and make judgments about the people. If you find yourself doing this, try to analyse which of your own needs you are meeting as you take sides or pass judgments.

Beware, too, of the temptation Christians have of trying to apply spiritual answers to such situations. If this committee all went away and prayed about it, would that in itself take them further forward? It might, but then again it might not. This question is not intended in any way to devalue the very meaningful and significant practice of prayer in a Christian community, but most of the committee feel their arguments are sound; unless they are aware of their real motives in putting forward these arguments, they will not be open to changing their positions. A great deal of rhetoric can result from trying to discern the will of God: 'Thy will be done, not ours'. To achieve this, and before they pray, the individuals concerned will have to reach, or be willing to reach, a personal detachment about the outcome of the discussion. It may be helpful to suggest to them that they examine honestly their own motives before God; that they work hard in prayer for God to show them how others on the committee feel; and that they try to give to God their particular desired outcome. What we are often tempted to do in such situations is to pray that God will change everyone else! Prayer might lead to some of the group making progress, but it is unlikely that any of them would get to that state of complete detachment without exploring further the gains and losses for those whom the decision will affect. It is our experience that sometimes it is the most vulnerable, like Sarah in this story, who give the most ground because they begin to feel guilty about meeting their own needs. Sometimes the guilt feeling may be appropriate, but it could also be irrational. To say the least, the situation is complex and calls for real wisdom and discernment.

It seems that there can be unintentional dishonesty around Christian groups concerning their motives in the context of decision-making. This is a misappropriation of Christian teaching resulting in people being 'nice' rather than truthful. This means that, even when we actually recognise our own motives and can privately acknowledge self-interest, we put our own needs, or even wants, first and may deny such motivation to others. We are afraid of our own weaknesses and most of us fear the judgment and rejection of others. To preach what ought to be done concerning, for example, self-denial presupposes that we are able to recognise when we are meeting our own needs or wants, and also that we have the capacity to deny ourselves in a particular situation.

It is also important to recognise that God created us with needs that he intended should be met. Thus, meeting our own needs is not necessarily wrong: it may be essential for our survival – physical, emotional, intellectual or spiritual. While we all require things such as food, warmth, rest and love, it is possible to overindulge ourselves on these. The issue is further complicated by the fact that needs differ, not only between individuals, but also for the same individual at different times in their lives. Some of us feel the cold more than others; many elderly people need more warmth than they used to when they were young.

> 'At one stage in my life, I put a great deal of effort into denying myself products made by firms who, I considered, exploited vulnerable groups in the world. During a time of considerable emotional trauma, all my energy was invested in surviving; doing any shopping at all took all my energy, and my former discrimination went by the board. My need to conserve energy in order to survive outweighed my need to serve the cause of justice.'
> (Pauline Bell)

To return to the Harvest sub-committee, there is never only one way of attempting to resolve conflict. One factor has not been given any weight in the discussion so far: those who gave the produce and those who paid for it at the auction did so in the belief that all the proceeds would go as usual to the elderly in the village. Would it be ethical, or even the correct procedure, for the committee to consider sending it elsewhere? Perhaps the issue should be under discussion for a future fund, but not the present one. The donors could then be advised in advance of where the money is to go. This would postpone the need for decisions. On this occasion, that could be helpful; at other times it simply avoids facing the conflict.

If Sarah were to share with the group how the loss of the hamper would affect her Christmas, her honesty and vulnerability might help the committee to resolve the conflict. This could be costly for Sarah, especially if she is not comfortable in the group. Keith could help her to do this by inviting her to share honestly and by affirming her openness.

These are only some suggestions. It is important to recognise that if people feel strongly about something, emotions can override reason. Sometimes to postpone the decision can be helpful, as long as the chairperson can offer a procedure for a future meeting which might help the group to arrive at a decision acceptable to all, even if not a consensus. In the following dialogue, we discuss some measures a chairperson might offer to a group to help them resolve a dilemma.

DIALOGUE

PB: The first thing that concerns me about the Harvest sub-committee is whether it has any ground rules for making decisions. Larger committees may have a constitution which sets guidelines about whether they decide by a vote or by consensus. How are the members of this particular group going to arrive at a decision? Do they know?

PJ: My feeling is that even if the main committee, of which they are a sub-committee, had a clear constitution – and it's not likely in a church context – a sub-committee would be much more informal. They probably have no clear ground rules, but they would try to act democratically.

PB: A group like this may feel that the church isn't a democracy, but about hearing God's will. Thus, the most appropriate way of reaching a decision would be to reach a consensus. However, that could cause problems and may lead to people who think differently not expressing their views for fear of rocking the boat. Insistence upon consensus can prevent people from thinking critically about the decisions being made.

PJ: There is also an opportunity for influential or dominant members to exert pressure. I was on a committee once when during the final discussion the chairperson said, 'I want a consensus on this.' That really put pressure on me not to rock the boat.

PB: Sometimes it's a group of people, a faction, that exerts pressure on the rest.

PJ: Yes, but whatever they decide, remember that it has to go back to the main committee (in this case), and they are going to be accountable for any decision that is made. If it's not a solid decision they will attract criticism, which will add to the conflict, not solve it. Another factor here is the unfortunate fact that they are 2:2, with the men on one side and the women on the other. That's not a healthy place to start! A straight vote would not solve anything, and they are so polarised that a genuine change of heart is unlikely.

PB: In that sort of power struggle, the chairperson is in an unenviable position, but he's also going to need a lot of skill to handle them. In Keith's case, he must know how they feel, and he needs to intervene *before* they get to a confrontation.

PJ: He could sound them out individually before they meet together, and get some sort of measure of where they're going. When he realises that they are on a collision course, he could try to take the confrontation out of it, perhaps by some form of group discussions. For instance, since they are 2:2, he could pair them, putting opposing opinions together, and ask them as a pair to draw up the advantages and disadvantages of *one* decision. Because they are on opposite sides, they will be made to look at both points of view and really listen as they work together.

Then the two pairs could come together and compare notes. If it's appropriate, they could repeat the exercise with the other decision so that it is seen as even-handed. At the end of it, they might have got away from the personalities involved and just be concentrating on the issues.

PB: A similar exercise would be to look at the *gains* and *losses* for those inside the group and for those outside it. Then they could ask questions like, 'Given the fact that some people in the village are going to lose in this way, do we really feel that this is the right decision?' Both these approaches might get them to see things from another's perspective. It would be even less likely to lead to confrontation if the small groups were to meet before the meeting, perhaps at home, and bring the results to the meeting.

PJ: Even so, the chairperson should not be afraid of having all the issues, and the feelings that go with them, brought into the open, as long as any ensuing conflict is creative rather than destructive, and as long as he is prepared to handle the emotion. They have to be brought out if the people are to be enabled towards reaching the most helpful decision.

PB: If we look at just one member of the group, Peter, we should remember that underneath what he is saying lies guilt about living so comfortably yet giving so little to the Third World. His motives arise out of that feeling. This is quite different from Sarah in that he, unlike her, has nothing to lose if the money goes out of the village. Yet neither of them is likely to own up to their emotions of guilt and fear unless they feel it is safe to do so. It is easy for Peter to use ethical arguments in this because he is working from theory; it's Sarah who will have to practise the sacrifice.

PJ: We can only guess what Peter's reaction would be if the chairperson succeeded in bringing all this out into the open. It may cause him to become more entrenched; he may become defensive; perhaps he is just blinkered about how people like Sarah actually live, and would be quite contrite if it were to be made plain to him.

PB: It would be a challenge for him to accept that he is expecting a sacrifice of Sarah that he is not making himself. It may be possible for the chairperson to get him to see this in general terms without bringing Sarah into it.

PJ: Keith, as chairperson and minister, might be skilled enough to create the sort of climate in the committee meeting where people feel safe to own their emotions. I know that sounds easy, but it isn't! It's part of the whole task he has, one which includes making sure that all the relevant information is known to the members so that they are able to make informed decisions.

PB: Also, it's important sometimes to be sure that people are arguing about the same things. If we broaden the discussion a bit, away from this example, in any committee there is always some desired end product – resolving some difficulty; bringing out something new; doing away with something unsatisfactory. Can we think of different problem-solving techniques which a group might use as part of a decision-making process?

PJ: One beginning might be a session of brainstorming, where all the possible ideas are contributed without any discussion at this stage, with everyone free to add something. The points are all written up for everyone to look at. It opens up ideas, whereas conflict closes them down.

PB: Yes, it has the merit of one idea building on another or combining with another, triggering another, and there is no evaluation until the brainstorm is completed.

PJ: Then as a group you can evaluate, put in order of priority, whatever you want, but at least you will have brought out all the implications. Many people find it non-threatening because it is a group activity.

PB: Another way to help decisions is to use a decision matrix. For example, if you were trying to decide to buy a piece of equipment, like a photocopier, you might make a list of criteria that are important for you in relation to the functions you want that machine to fulfil within the church, and then rate the different machines on a ten-point scale. I guess this process is for decisions that are fairly clear-cut, not complex; if you're dealing with ideas and values it's much more difficult to use this approach. A matrix is a logical process.

PJ: I can see how that would help by getting away from personalities.

PB: Another way which can be helpful is to ask whether the problem that appears to be the trigger is really the main issue. For instance, our Harvest sub-committee is looking at something quite narrow; it may be more productive to address the question of how they as a church or village community help both their own elderly people *and* those in the Third World, looking at the many different ways of doing that. This would enable people to work with all the creative ideas possible, rather than to protect their own viewpoints.

PJ: So a chairperson has to have quite a repertoire of skills from which to select, according to what is appropriate and where the group is.

PB: It's not possible ever to prevent people holding different viewpoints, and one wouldn't want to do that anyway.

PJ: No. All these different views need to be valued so that together they can explore what everybody believes and they can use it to make progress. Without differences of opinion, they won't make progress: they'll just be 'yes' men and women.

PB: That's about valuing diversity and seeing it as creative, and encouraging the group to have that kind of mindset, rather than reacting to people when they express a different opinion.

PJ: It does seem that a great deal is expected of a chairperson.

PB: It's very easy for those of us in the church to want to believe we are being totally altruistic and open to the will of God. In doing so we often deny not only our sinfulness but also our humanity. All of us have genuine needs just as we have real emotions, and we need to try for ourselves to encourage one another to look at what each of us is going to get from a particular decision – what needs we are meeting for ourselves – and whether we can be open to exploring the appropriateness of those needs.

CHAPTER 3

CONFLICTING THEOLOGY

How do you see God?

■ From the words listed below, choose the *one* that best expresses the way you predominantly see or feel about God. Do not think about it too much; go for the quick emotional response. Beware especially of responding as you think you *ought*; this is not a theology examination or a test for orthodoxy.

Judge	Guide	Master
Father	Friend	Companion
Potter	Creator	Teacher
Rescuer	King	Mother
Sustainer	Foreman	Line Manager
Consultant	Advisor	Captain
Shepherd	Protector	Counsellor
Prison Warder		Leader
Probation Officer		

■ Think about your choice. What does it say about your thoughts and feelings about God?

- Do you reflect your chosen image of God in the way you relate to others? For example, if you see God as Master are you masterful? If you see God as Protector are you protective?
- Does your image of God reflect your leadership style or your expectations of those in leadership or management positions?
- If people with predominantly different images of God sit on the same committee, how might this affect their expectations of the procedures the group might use when trying to make decisions?
- What does the fact that different people in the church hold predominantly different images of God mean for the decision-making committee?

In some churches there is a belief that, when making decisions, a group should be able, by honouring the guidelines found in the Bible and through the work of the Holy Spirit, to arrive at consensus. This is seen as discerning the will of God. After all, the Holy Spirit can't lead seven people to one decision and three to another . . . or can he? There are many areas in life where Christians over the centuries would claim the authority of God for their particular stance.

Take two Christians, George and Tina, who are engaged in debate over the biblical justification for war. George recognises the fact of a fallen world and the presence of evil. War, and therefore large-scale killing of other human beings, is a last resort, but may be the lesser of two evils in the face of an aggressor prepared to enforce violent oppression on all in his path. Tina, however, argues that the kingdom of God embodies fully the concept of *shalom* – peace with God, humanity and self – and advocates the beating of swords into ploughshares and weapons into surgical instruments for the sick. Who is right? On the surface it looks as if they are in opposition, and that only one or other viewpoint can be right. However, is it possible that, in some way or other, both represent the will of God? Either argument represents an aspect of the truth: Tina's stance serves as a brake to the potential excesses of those who would fight a just cause; George's argument helps everyone to take seriously the imperfections of the world.

However, the two positions present a kind of counter-tension. God is a God of paradox but can he be inconsistent? Can he really lead Christian people in different directions in the same circumstances and at the same time? Maybe he could lead individuals facing conscription differently, but is it also possible he could lead differently those trying to decide whether to give £727 to the elderly living in the parish or to those in poorer parts of the world? Can he be calling Colin to leadership and a preaching ministry in the local church and at the same time be calling Tom to remove him from that ministry?

This may seem unlikely but in some circumstances could be a possibility. If a large sum of money is to be spent on local church amenities, a dissenting

51

voice drawing attention to the needs of the poor may well serve as a warning not to neglect responsibilities in that direction. God is the God of process who can use anyone and any situation. In the dispute over the allocation of Harvest money in Chapter two, God may be prompting those on one side to be more aware of the needs of elderly people in the locality and, at the same time, those on the other side to take action on behalf of the poor in other cultures.

However, whether this is the God of grace at work guiding people differently or whether it is the redemption of people's imperfections is open to discussion. We would want to question seriously the ability of a small group of people to put aside their prejudices, needs, emotions, partial understandings of the Bible and past experiences, in order to arrive at total consensus concerning the will of God on issues like extending the church or buying a new set of hymn books.

This is not to suggest that people are being deliberately obtuse or refusing to respond to God's will, but rather to be realistic about the fallen nature of humanity. None of us can understand God in his completeness; we see him 'through a glass darkly', partly because God has chosen not to reveal all, but also because our knowledge and experience are incomplete and limited about the things God has revealed. It is not possible for us to be 'empty vessels'; we can make decisions by putting the facts before us through a Christian filter, but even that filter is in some way unique to the individual. If, like Chris on the Harvest sub-committee, we have had experience of working in a poorer culture, we cannot deny that experience when making decisions about where the Harvest Festival proceeds should go.

Similarly, we can be deeply influenced by our image of God and by particular sections of the Bible. If we see God as Guide or as Master, then we will expect to get clear directions from him. It is probable that we *will* get them, perhaps through a verse or chapter, or in some other way that we recognise as a word from God. If on the other hand we see God as a father with whom we have a good relationship and to whom we can relate as an adult son or daughter, we may feel we have more freedom to make a decision in the light of the known facts. Those who believe in a God who gives clear guidance on all issues will expect the committee to spend time praying and listening to God together; those who have another kind of relationship with God may feel that 'God is in my thinking' and that the pros and cons of a situation should be weighed before coming to any decision.

There are churches where the culture embraces an expectation that God will reveal his will in quite specific, or supernatural, ways in certain situations. The exercise of charismatic gifts can be greatly encouraging to others and lead to deep experiences of God. However, it is possible in conflict situations for these gifts to be used in highly manipulative ways. There are people who, when emotionally affected by a conflict, become very vulnerable. It is not unusual for another person involved to have 'a word from the

Lord' purporting to throw light or guidance on the situation. We would not want to deny this may be true. But when someone makes this claim, it can be as a means of bolstering their self-confidence, giving weight to their argument and convincing others that they have got it right. It is quite hard for those they are opposing to challenge this, and if people are struggling to be open and are finding the conflict painful, it can be used as a means of delivering an unfair blow – hitting below the belt. In such cultures, a prophecy has more credibility than 'I think we should . . .' There may be no deliberate intention to manipulate, but that can be the result. Both of us have had involvement in churches like these and this has been our experience.

Similarly, a strong commitment on the part of leaders to particular passages or ideas in the Bible can also fuel the conflict. One might be in a church which places great emphasis on the authority of the overall leader. If the leader supports the image of God as King, this may affect the style of leadership and be supported by references to the Bible about the authority given to leadership. Any dissenting voices, such as Colin's and those who supported him, can be quickly silenced by the leader who takes his stand on his authority as God's appointed leader in the church. Again, this is not to deny that people have authority and power, but to challenge the way such power is used, particularly in conflict situations where others are vulnerable.

Those who see God as a friend may suggest that,

since the Bible expects all of us to be growing towards maturity and that Paul even instructed leaders 'to present every person mature in Christ', a more appropriate way of handling a conflict would be to say 'talk about this, adult to adult'.

To sum up: however ideal the concept of consensus in decision making and conflict situations, it may be quite liberating to recognise that lack of consensus may be a healthy counter-tension, a gift from God. What seems like consensus could, in reality, be a case of subtle manipulation and a cover-up for conflict or the oppression of individuals.

We would go so far as to suggest that highly cohesive groups should avoid making premature decisions, because such decisions may be the result of 'group think', based on information or ideas which confirm existing values or beliefs. Speedy decisions can preclude a critical appraisal of alternatives, which could result in a decision being made which is less than the best in the circumstances.

Recourse to authority in leaders, or to what is written in the Bible, is important; but leaders and followers, as well as theologians of all kinds or conditions, can filter things through their own Christian understanding and experience to arrive at different conclusions, about doctrine or about decisions. Sometimes it may be possible to agree to differ and accept a majority decision; at other times a separation, as in the case of Paul and Barnabas, may be the most creative way forward.

All of this is to fall short of God's perfection.

Certainly, Christians are called upon to seek unity, but not uniformity. And it must be a real unity, which cannot be arrived at by asking people to be dishonest or by manipulating them. Sometimes it is possible to experience unity as Christians whilst being in conflict over an issue, though this is rare. Usually the most powerful in a church, often the leaders, find ways of removing the dissenting voices. People who disagree may be asked to leave, or told to repent or submit. Unwillingness to do this is judged as rebellion and they are either excommunicated or made to feel they have no choice but to go. This was Colin's experience, but it is not unknown for a divorced vicar to be hounded out of the church in which he is working, all in the name of God's will.

If our dominant image is of God as Judge, we will probably be judgmental of others who hold views or are in situations which we discern to be contrary to the will of God. If our dominant image is of the Good Shepherd, then we are more likely to favour forgiving and supporting those who, in our perception, have made mistakes. This we see as the will of God.

Throughout Christian history, conflicting theology has been a regular source of dissension and division. Whilst referring to the Bible and honestly seeking to understand and respond to its meaning, all of us when involved in conflict situations need to exercise great care that we do not use it metaphorically to beat one another over the head. We should also seek to avoid using the Bible in a way which manipulates those who for whatever reason are the most vulnerable.

There are issues around today, like the ordination of women and inter-faith worship, which are creating both discussion and conflict between theologians on all sides. In local congregations different theologies continue to give rise to differences of opinion and practice about worship, the use of spiritual gifts, leadership, and use of buildings, as well as about the meaning of evangelism and mission. Different groups within the same church may use tradition or the Bible to justify their position. These groups may find it helpful to listen to the other side with openness and to explore conflicting needs and values as well as theology.

Given the fact that each denomination in Britain claims to have a biblical model of leadership (in some cases the claim is *the* biblical model of leadership), and that the variations range from ordained stipendiary men to groups of lay elders both male and female, we need to acknowledge the difficulties of being dogmatic. Such leadership structures are related to a theology of the church which may be most simplistically separated into those who believe certain men are called or singled out from their peers to the priesthood and those who believe that all Christians, men and women, form the priesthood of all believers. These differences and conflicts have been around for hundreds of years. The theological stance that individuals take on this issue will affect their expectations of style in leaders. It is conflicting leadership and followership styles that we explore in the next chapter.

CHAPTER 4

CONFLICTING LEADERSHIP/ FOLLOWERSHIP STYLES

During the reign of Solomon, the wealth and splendour of Jerusalem was achieved at the expense of the people. Vast building projects were undertaken by forced labour, though the King did stop short of making slaves of the Israelites. During his reign, there was considerable unrest and a rebellion was led by Jeroboam who, when his life was threatened, fled to Egypt. Although Solomon was successful at generating wealth, his leadership style was undoubtedly authoritarian and oppressive for many.

When Solomon died, he was succeeded by his son, Rehoboam, who was soon confronted by a sizeable deputation led by Jeroboam.

■ **Read 1 Kings 12:1–5 only.**

For three days, he consulted with the elders who had served his father and the young men who had grown

59

up with him.

> ■ You may or may not know the outcome of the story, but imagine you are a member of one of the groups consulted.
> ■ How will you answer? Why will you answer in that way?
> ■ What risks are involved for Rehoboam if he takes your advice?
> ■ If you do not know the rest of the story, how do you think he responded to the advice given by the two groups?

> ■ Read 1 Kings 12:6–20 to find out.

In this chapter we want to suggest that there are different leadership styles and different followership styles. It may be that as you read you are able to identify your own style.

Leadership is a popular topic for Christian publishers and a great deal has already been researched and written about different leadership styles, though very little on followership styles. We do not intend here to enter the debate about whether one particular leadership style is more appropriate for local churches than another; nor do we wish to become involved in whether one style is more Biblical or more Christian than another. Our concern is rather to explore how leadership and followership styles lead to or influence conflict situations in churches.

For the purposes of this discussion, we are going to use as a tool for analysis the three styles of leadership which originated in the research done by Lewin, Lippett and White[1]. These have been variously adapted and re-labelled. We shall refer to them as

- authoritarian
- enabling
- non-directive

A leader with a legitimate leadership role such as a minister in a church, who has a tendency to make or want to make all the decisions, is *authoritarian* in style. Such leaders are holding onto as much power as possible within an organisation.

The *enabling* style gives power away. Other members of the community are allowed to influence decisions and to carry out many of the leadership functions within that community.

The *non-directive* leader uses little or no power to influence the community. Leadership and initiative, as well as decisions and ways of working, have to come from others.

If leadership is being analysed using this approach, it may be helpful to see a continuum rather than three fixed styles. So some leaders may be identified as being enabling, but might be on the continuum a few points towards the authoritarian rather than towards the non-directive. This also assumes that leaders have a preferential style, either by virtue of personality or by choice; that is, generally speaking, they operate in one of the three styles. If they have awareness, they may for a specific decision or purpose choose to adopt a different style. Returning to the exercise in Chapter three, where readers were invited to choose their image of God and think about whether they reflected that image in their own relationships, we would suggest that there is frequently in the church a correlation between preferred leadership styles and their image of God; those whose image of God is that of King or Master will prefer a more direct authoritarian leadership than will those whose image of God is Friend or Counsellor. This latter group will prefer a more enabling style. These tendencies would be true whether the people concerned are leaders or followers.

The authoritarian style is fairly traditional and represented in the Catholic and Anglo-Catholic church by the priest as father and presumably the congregation as children. However, in more recent times this style can also be seen in churches where submission to those in leadership is strongly emphasised. This leadership is sometimes corporate in that it rests with a small group of elders and not necessarily in one person, though often there is an 'apostle' or some other leader in the background. The authoritarian style leads to a community based on a hierarchical model. The overall leader will be at the top of the pyramid, with the possibility of perhaps a few being in some kind of middle-management positions; the majority of the congregation will be at the base of the pyramid.

The enabling style of leadership delegates power and some other functions, so that tasks are performed through a variety of small groups which may be clustered round a central leadership group, such as a group of deacons, elders or the PCC. With this style of leadership, opportunity is offered to group members to give leadership through contributing ideas and skills in relation to the group's task, as well as performing group maintenance functions (see Chapter ten).

The non-directive style is rarely seen as a basic style for leading a church. Occasionally, in an attempt to get others to take responsibility, a leader may opt out of giving any kind of direction because he believes that the group has acquired an unhealthy dependency or because, in a missionary context, they are working themselves out of a job. This strategy would normally be for a short-term, specific purpose only.

A change of leadership, particularly if it involves a change of style, can lead to conflict. A congregation which has been without a minister for a while and has been running its own affairs will, for example, have in its midst those who would immediately react to an authoritarian leader. There may of course also be others who would welcome this style, which would create the potential for the 'for' and 'against' factions.

A congregation in a city suburb composed of mostly professional people carrying managerial responsibility in their everyday work will probably have an expectation of skilled enabling leadership.

They will expect efficiency and such things as agendas for meetings. A truly inner-city congregation, on the other hand, may be looking for more direction, but will not necessarily want anything that smacks of bureaucratic procedures.

A leader very different from his predecessor will meet with mixed fortunes, resented by those who dislike the change of style and applauded by those who appreciate it.

Where a leader adopts a leadership style out of choice and because of particular values, he may find himself going against the prevailing culture, which could lead to problems. To be enabling in a feudal culture may cause conflict; for example, Vinay Samuel and Chris Sugden write:

> The Asian tradition is one of deference to others who are older, wiser and appointed by the destiny of birth allowing them to determine the course of other people's lives ... Sadly, churches are often affected by the feudalistic pattern of leadership so powerful in surrounding society.[2]

It is important to note that it may be wholly constructive to confront the culture or expectations of any church. Growth may be the result of such conflict. However, it may also be important to be cautious, when changing or confronting expectations concerning leadership style, that the leader is not confronting the status quo too soon, so that people become resistant to change rather than open to it. Such conflict can be destructive to all concerned.

No leadership style will suit every individual in a community. Followers also have different styles;[3]

■ The *deferential* follower sees the leader as the expert with the 'vision' and the answers.

■ The *distancing* follower does not want to be influenced by the leadership, but rather wants to maintain some kind of authority over her own life. She is not going to commit herself or get involved.

■ The *independent* follower is a thinker. He looks and weighs, is more concerned with questions than with answers, and is usually on to the next question before resolving the previous one. This type of follower is usually an intellectual.

■ The *collegiate* follower is one who prefers to be regarded, probably because of professional considerations, as a co-worker.

■ The *performance* follower judges success or achievement by quantity, usually in a fairly simplistic way. He is the one who sees the church as needing *more* Bible studies, *more* missions and *more* prayer.

All kinds of clashes are possible between leadership style and followership style.

Before we look at this in more detail you may like to try making a matrix of the two:

On a sheet of A4 paper, draw up a grid with the three leadership styles at the top and the five followership styles down the left hand side. At each intersection, write in either a comment or a score about the probability of success or conflict. For example, the first one will be the authoritarian leader with the deferential follower.

Much of what is often labelled 'personality clash' can be explained in terms of the interaction between leadership style and followership style. The authoritarian leader and deferential follower are likely to get on very well, but the same leader with a distancing or independent follower may experience all kinds of problems. The collegiate follower can be a threat to an overall leader and conflict can result from frustration. Similarly, if the collegiate follower is at first accepted and then becomes a threat and is dropped, serious conflict may follow. The performance follower may well be frustrated by an enabling type leader, particularly if that leader is towards the non-directive end of the continuum. Not only will an authoritarian leader clash with an independent follower, but a deferential follower and an independent follower sitting on the same committee might also frequently clash because their expectations of the leader as well as of the organisation or church will be very different. Two leaders in a church with different styles may also find themselves in conflict over ways of doing things.

So far in this discussion we have assumed that the designated leaders are really those doing the leading in the community. This may not always be the case, and many of us have heard joking references to, and even had experience of, the 'power behind the throne'. Women married to members of an all male leadership group may have a great deal of power in the making of decisions. Sometimes it is an ex-senior colleague who is viewed by the leader as a guru. Or it might be a particular church warden who has been in office for years and who may be powerful enough to lead by blocking.

Scenarios such as these can make differences flare into destructive conflict very quickly. If the person in leadership is afraid of conflict, and has a powerful person close to him, issues cannot be tackled with any openness or honesty. The most obvious literary example is the complexity that arose in Anthony Trollope's 'Barchester Chronicles' when the bishop's wife was actually running the diocese from the parlour or the bedroom, rather than the bishop running it from his study. She was the power behind the throne and his fear of her reactions was the most powerful feature in any decisions he made.

This raises the major issue in this section, that of *power*. French and Raven[4] have developed five concepts about the bases of interpersonal influence:

- *Legitimate* power is exerted by those seen by others as having the right to be influential.

- *Reward* power depends upon the advantages or 'favours' a person is perceived as being able to give.
- *Coercive* power carries with it the threat of punishment.
- *Expert* power depends upon the knowledge and skill a person is seen as possessing.
- *Referent* power comes from being in close relationship with the source of power, perhaps a leader whose preferred style is authoritarian. It has to do with feeling recognised, known and valued by the leader.

Church ministers are always given legitimate power. By some process they are chosen for leadership and will be formally acknowledged as a legitimate leader through some kind of public ceremony. Without this legitimacy, they are unlikely to be recognised or accepted by their congregations. On the other hand, legitimate power alone may not be sufficient for them to have real influence, and if a congregation ultimately rejects a legitimate leader, that leader usually has to resign because he will be leading in name only or in limited areas.

Reward power is meted out through approval or through being invited to take on some position of responsibility which is in the gift of the leaders. An example would be home group leader.

Coercive power is used to ignore those the leader disapproves of, so that responsibility and particular roles are withheld. Where the style of leadership is authoritarian, coercive power can be used to try to persuade people to conform. We know of an incident when the leaders of one church threatened to put two people out of membership if they did not stop seeing one another.

In looking at expert power, there is some evidence that teachers, for example, prefer principals who use expert or referent power. Our hypothesis is that this is also generally true of congregations in local churches. Two people have shared with us recently that they left their local church because the vicar never spoke to them; he spoke only to his 'in' group. If this claim is true, this leader is using referent power with some of the congregation but not with others. Those in the 'out group' feel left out because he does not refer to them and therefore they do not feel valued.

Expert power is a complex issue. Congregations who perceive their minister or leaders as the theological expert can develop or stay in a state of dependence which can stunt the working out of theology within their own contexts and situations. They rely on the minister to do this. On the other hand, much conflict that we have come across in the local church stems from the lack of skill in managing what is really a complex organisation, a lack of real management expertise. This is more likely to cause conflict where there are people in the congregation who do possess this kind of expertise, both in situations where such people are willing to use their gifts but are not given the chance to do so, and where they exercise no responsibility by choice but feel they suffer from incompetent management.

The whole issue can be further complicated by virtue of power struggles within a leadership group, whatever the style of leadership. In one parish church, the vicar, an authoritarian style leader, decided that a sum of money given to the church should be used to purchase a Marian statue. Someone working for a Christian organisation, who was a collegiate style follower and had been supportive of and committed to the vicar, felt this was an unhelpful, autocratic decision since the statue was to be imposed on the congregation. The PCC was divided, but a small majority decided to apply for a faculty. The faculty was refused but the statue was displayed anyway. The congregation began to divide. The collegiate follower and his partner left the church and others followed them. This is a misuse of power, a lack of expert power, and the outcome is a power struggle.

Finally, let us return to the case study of the first chapter and look at that through the lens of conflicting leadership/followership styles.

Tom was a leader exercising *legitimate* power as the vicar. He chose after a year to share that leadership and power with a group which included Colin. Tom therefore moved into an *enabling* style of leadership, at least on the surface. It could be that his basic style was *authoritarian*, but that he had been led to believe that an enabling style was more biblical. The conflict was fuelled by the confusing, not to say totally conflicting, messages his action over Colin gave to the rest of the team. Without any discussion he acted in an authoritarian manner, even though they were supposed to be sharing the leadership. The team's power was snatched from them and, having relinquished something of his own legitimate power, Tom chose unilaterally to take it back. Regardless of the issue of Colin, this was really what was fanning the flames of conflict.

Colin himself was in a *collegiate* followership role as the licensed lay reader. Apart from the shock of finding Tom using *coercive* power against him, he suddenly finds himself not only feeling a victim of injustice but also being expected to become a *deferential* follower, as indeed were the rest of the team when they were instructed to submit to leadership.

Tom's lack of expertise right from the beginning in handling the situation contributed to the conflict. *Expert* power was lacking, described by some of the leadership as pastoral ineptness. His lack of skill ensured that the conflict ran on to its destructive end.

The grid on page 72 is intended to summarise some of the discussion in this chapter where the focus has been on differing styles of leading and following which in fact leads to differing ways of handling conflict. Leaders and followers can co-operate or collude to handle conflict in any of these ways.

In the light of the discussion on leadership and followership styles, you might like to consider which styles would put individuals where on this grid, when differences surface in a group or organisation.

CONFLICT RESOLUTION GRID

PERSON/GROUP MAINTENANCE

HIGH

1:9 **Smoothing over**
Surface harmony must be maintained. The anxious pretence to maintain things as they are not. Self-deception abounds.

Problem solving **9:9**
All parties agree to search for best solution. Emotions, facts, doubts are owned, faced, confronted and explored together. Maturity abounds.

Compromising
5:5
The search for workable solutions. Negotiation, give and take. No winners/losers. Accommodation abounds.

Withdrawing
See no conflict, hear no conflict, speak no conflict. Means differences do not **1:1** have to be dealt with. Avoidance abounds.

Compelling
Leadership authoritatively suppresses conflict. Followers are to obey. Win/lose power struggles occur. **9:1** Coercion abounds.

LOW **TASK CENTRED** **HIGH**

Adapted from Blake & Mouton, *The Fifth Achievement*, 1971.

In the case studies in this book so far:

Tom moved between withdrawing and compelling.

Jim, the new steward, used a similar pattern in his handling of the conflict with Ada. Through withdrawing he forced the situation he had created to remain in place, though he failed to stand on his authority openly.

The Harvest sub-committee led by Keith was left with the possibility of compromising or problem-solving. Some individuals on the committee might have wanted to withdraw or to smooth things over, but given the personalities in that group it seems unlikely that the entire committee would collude in this way.

At this point, it might be helpful to think of a situation which occurred in a group in your church which led to differences being expressed, and to identify, using the grid, how that situation was tackled.

REFERENCES

1 Lewin K, Lippit R & White R K, 'Patterns of aggressive behaviour in experimentally created 'social climates' in *Journal of Social Psychology*, 1939, pp 10, 271–299.
2 Vinay Samuel & Chris Sugden in *Christianity a World Faith*, Keeley R, Lion, 1985, p 185.
3 Based on unpublished research done by Cliff Hayward, Scripture Union Training Unit.
4 Cited by Schmuck R & Schmuck P, in *Group Process in the Classroom*, WCB, 1979, 3rd edition.

CHAPTER 5

CONFLICTING EMOTIONS

> ■ Think about an experience of conflict in the local church that you have been involved in and list any **emotions** you felt or that you recognised in others.
> ■ Reflect on the case studies and scenarios mentioned in previous chapters and list any **emotions** that are, or appear to be, around.
> ■ Note any similarities.

If only feelings and emotions were not involved in conflict situations, everything would be straightforward. On the other hand, things would often be less destructive if we could all acknowledge the emotions that we feel, first of all to ourselves and then to others.

Churches can be very unhealthy places as far as emotions are concerned. Somehow or other we manage to distort the Christian gospel to the point where we often attempt to live in relationship and community in a way that might be described as 'nice', but which certainly is not real or honest. This in no way denies the call to strive for unity in community or that there is a rigorous demand to grow and change in order to become increasingly more Christ-like, living out qualities generally recognised as the fruit of the Spirit. Despite some of the translations we have of the Bible, this cannot be superimposed; it has to come from the inside out.

The Bible has a high regard for honesty and truth in relationships. Honesty and truth cannot be present unless there is also trust. In David Augsburger's helpful commentary on 1 John 1:5–10, he points out that John's central images are:

> **light** (open, clear, acceptant, revealed, self-disclosed)
> **darkness** (denial, deceit, alienation, hate, hiddenness)

Additionally, he examines descriptions of the relationships John is picturing in his drama:

> **God** is light. Open, clear, acceptant, revealing light who has self-disclosed in Jesus (vs 1–3).
> **We** can step out of the darkness and join one another in this open, clear, acceptant circle of self-disclosing people who follow Jesus (v 7).[1]

Does this sound like your committee, PCC, deacons, elders or stewards in their meetings? Augsburger goes on to say:

> So we try to build false communities based on faking, feigning and fooling, but the quality of common-life, community, communion of heart touching heart is lost in the charade.[2]

This way of relating is the way we are 'nice' to one another.

Two dominant emotions that are found in most conflict situations are *fear* and *anger*. When these emotions are present they are often suppressed by the individual herself, and rarely expressed to others in the group.

In our first case study, fear appears to have played some part in the decisions Tom made. The background of criticism from the congregation over Colin's marital situation which triggered his actions probably stemmed from Tom's fear of not giving the right leadership. Colin himself would fear losing his place in the church. Similarly, Ada feared losing her position when she was replaced as tea-maker. Jim was afraid of failing or losing credibility in the whole organisation of the Bank Holiday event. In the case of the Harvest Festival sub-committee, Sarah was afraid of losing her much-valued Christmas hamper, Nancy of losing votes, Keith of being an inadequate chairman and not enabling the group to resolve the situation.

Fear gets an even firmer grip if people become entrenched in their opinions. It may be a deeply felt set of values, assumptions, traditions or practices that they are fearful of losing, but they can also become fearful of losing the argument or of losing face. This kind of fear can have a vice-like grip on a group and can lessen the possibility of people moving towards other positions. It is important to remember that feelings are not rational, and fear can in varying degrees paralyse our rational processes so that we stop hearing what other people are really saying. If we are really threatened we may even close down part of our thinking processes. Responses become emotional, but not necessarily honestly emotional. The real feeling can be suppressed or masked by appeals to higher authority – God, the Bible, another leader. Attack is said to be a good way of defence. Very rarely is someone honest enough to own that he is, at heart, afraid.

The other key emotion, anger, is a spontaneous reaction which can be absorbed or vented. Discharged anger can be used constructively or destructively, but it can also be displaced when the anger is channelled onto someone or something else: the angry deacon goes home and kicks the cat; the angry PCC member goes home and snaps at her husband. Destructive anger is anger which is unskilfully discharged so that it closes down discussion rather than leaving things open. It is easy to get into this kind of situation if we feel hurt because such feelings draw to the surface the desire to blame and to hurt back.

We do have a choice whether or not to deal with our anger. In a situation like a meeting, when an individual feels that spontaneous rush of anger, it may be helpful to own up to it openly rather than suppress it. In a group where there is genuine trust and a desire to listen, the group could then support the person concerned by accepting his or her feelings and by exploring the needs, expectations and hopes which are being threatened or ignored by the subject under discussion.

In a situation like the one in the first case study, where events are protracted and lengthy, emotions like anger play an increasingly dominant role. People feel angry with one another and self-esteem takes a battering, particularly when people perceive injustice. Overwhelming feelings of powerlessness, panic, fear, grief and loss all fuel the anger, impatience and frustration. With these kinds of feelings, affecting an individual so deeply, prayer can often be extremely difficult if not impossible. Individuals cannot find God in this experience, and anger may be directed as much towards him as towards others. There is sometimes a progression of desperation, barrenness and emptiness.

In such situations, individuals will almost certainly need help from a third party to sort out their emotions by reflecting on the specific experience, and to find ways of integrating it into their whole life experience. This may mean counselling.

If the conflict is really at a high pitch, a mediator or facilitator may be needed to help all the parties concerned individually and together. They need to identify the issues, the needs and expectations, the hopes for themselves and for the church; they also need to identify the source of the hurt and anger and ultimately share the hurt and anger with one another. We believe that failure to understand the importance of emotion, particularly anger, contributes to the breakdown.

Even when this process is agreed to and undertaken, however skilful the facilitator or mediator, it is still possible that the conflict will not be resolved. The pain for one or more of the people involved may be so deep that they cannot cope with making themselves vulnerable to those they perceive as causing their hurt. Yet others may be so sure that they are right that they are not open to changing their position, or they may feel that to do so would compromise truth. When one side holds to this belief, reconciliation is in doubt; if both sides feel it, then true resolution is extremely unlikely.

Similarly, when anger is discharged in a very aggressive way, it is difficult, almost in proportion to the strength of the perceived 'attack', for the 'defendant' to make himself vulnerable to the attacker. Whatever Jesus meant by 'turning the other cheek', it is a standard few of us in church groups have the maturity to practice in situations of intense emotional pain and stress towards those in the group we feel are our persecutors.

Sometimes a parting of the ways is the least destructive alternative if there is to be emotional healing. One way of looking at this is suggested by Robin Green[3] who wrote about the dynamics at work in a community which will lead to some people, or an individual, being made into scapegoats. Sometimes one person brings to the surface the pain and conflict that others have been suppressing, and that individual becomes the one chosen to carry it away into the wilderness. It is this act which enables healing to take place in the community left behind, and it may also be the only way the scapegoat can find sufficient space and calm to know healing.

In the following dialogue we explore some of the issues that arose when trying to handle emotions in a conflict situation. It may be helpful for the reader to think back to the exercise at the beginning of this chapter.

DIALOGUE

PB: In the case of the conflict between Tom and Colin, emotions were running so high, not only for the two of them but also for the rest of the leadership team, that there wasn't anyone with sufficient freedom from emotional stress to be able to help the situation by helping them to communicate. Because everyone was involved, there was no one left to play any kind of conciliatory role.

PJ: I suppose that's always the problem when the whole church is involved in that way. It's very different when it's a conflict over one specific issue, like the situation between Ada and Jim; the emotions are theirs. There must be somebody else in that church who could mediate between them. It might be the minister, but it could be anybody who has the skill to deal with Ada's emotion and Jim's insecurities, and help them to handle the emotions of the situation.

PB: Having the skill is the 'crunch', but it's not just that. Others may be aware that emotions are around, but no one may feel they have the authority to take it on, or that it's their responsibility; and of course some people would feel either that they didn't have the skill or that they were interfering.

PJ: That's true, but I still think that most people, if they saw two members of their church so locked into their emotions that they couldn't resolve a conflict, would want to do something to try to resolve it, whatever their level of skill. This might be on the simple level of trying to get Ada and Jim to recognise their own feelings, to see the situation from each other's point of view. Maybe a third party could ask them for suggestions about how the situation might be resolved and then explore that separately, before bringing them together.

PB: The success of that would depend on how skilled they were – unskilled intervention can be seen as meddling and can make the situation worse. I think that at this point we can only focus on a leader or a chairperson of some kind, of a home group or committee, where the task of handling emotions is part of the job. Their skills would be available to Ada and Jim. But for the purposes of our discussion here, let's keep to coping with what happens in a group.

PJ: I agree. It's usually when people meet together in groups that emotions become evident. Then whoever is in charge has to be able to handle them.

PB: Well, we can talk about the kind of things that a group leader can do to enable emotion to be handled more openly, and just give some pointers to ways in which they might do this.

PJ: People are only likely to express emotion openly if they feel they trust the group, and it is very much the role of the group leader to build up an environment of trust.

PB: This is sometimes acknowledged in contexts like home groups, where time is given to help people to relate to one another and to increase the levels of trust between the group members. I'm not sure that is always taken on board in relation to committee groups, such as PCCs, where there tends to be a focus very much on the task to be done, and a neglect of any kind of work on the thing that oils the wheels. So it is often less likely that foundations are put down to enable the group to handle feelings in a committee than in a home group; but even in the home group things can be very task orientated – you know the kind of thinking which says, 'We are here to study the Bible.' That's important, but sometimes not enough time is invested in helping people to relate.

PJ: What happens then when you have a group where people feel it is not all right to express emotion?

PB: People are not always conscious that this is the kind of environment they are in; our British culture and our church culture traditionally don't allow for much expression of feeling. There is one model of explaining this, that sees the group or committee as being a bit like an iceberg, seven eighths below the surface and just one eighth above. The seven eighths is seen as what is going on under the surface of any group. Sometimes that is OK but sometimes it isn't and unless some things are actually brought to the surface, it can impede the work of the group. If it is strong feelings about what the group is discussing or exploring, and they continue to stay beneath the surface, then they are in some way going to cause the group to dysfunction. Somebody will blow a fuse in the end, or people will go totally silent because they are repressing feelings. These unexpressed feelings will prevent the group getting on with the task. But in most situations in our society, the group or committee doesn't normally help people to express their feelings as they surface, and so people handle strong feelings in these two extreme ways, either suppressing or exploding – or alternating between the two. When this happens nothing is ever resolved.[4]

PJ: If some people are repressing and some people aren't, then the people who aren't are going to dominate the group, and they may be the more aggressive element in the group anyway. That will cause an imbalance in the true representation of what is happening in the group. People might find themselves swept along by those who are showing all the feeling and emotion and who are dominating; they may be afraid to speak out.

PB: Yes, or people just feel steam-rollered.

PJ: So this is very much about the sensitivity of the chairperson.

PB: In any group, whoever is taking on the role of leading or chairing needs to be sensitive about where people are on the emotional level, or at least it needs to be a question at the back of her mind. There needs to be a willingness to try to bring out into the open anything that you actually observe; so, an example of that would be if there is a person in the group who usually makes contributions to discussion and who has gone totally silent, then it could be helpful to say to him, 'You're very quiet, Bill. What do you feel about this?' In some instances it might be more appropriate to do this outside the meeting or between meetings and, if necessary or helpful, to bring it back to the group next time.

PJ: Is reading body language something that all the group could benefit from, not just the chairperson? If members of the committee were sensitive to each other, they too should be more aware of how people are feeling. It would be good if at least some of the group could have some training in recognising the signs of 'feelings' in others and be given the freedom to say, 'You haven't contributed, Sam. Do you want to say something about the way the discussion is going?'

PB: I'd love to see groups working in that way, but maybe it needs to start with the group leader. Whoever it is who responds to body language, they need to be careful that in doing so they comment only on what they see and don't try to interpret, so if someone is wringing her hands we comment on that fact and we don't interpret that action by suggesting what it means. We then give them space to express feeling if it's there.

PJ: That's an important distinction. You have to check out body language because it is so easy to be wrong; you might see a certain facial expression and assume the person is angry, whereas in fact it could be one of any number of other emotions – or even a twinge of backache! The important thing is that you have noticed something is being triggered; you can't assume anything until you have asked about it.

PB: I think the other chairing skill, particularly if it is a decision-making group or a task group of some kind, is a chairperson or leader keeping the pace steady, so that when the proposal is made, space is given to allow people to say how they feel as well as what they think about that proposal. If it is a significant or controversial proposal, this is vital, as a quick intervention from a very strong character can quickly lead to polarisation of opinion.

PJ: This happens too when people say things that take us by surprise.

PB: You mean like in the home group context when somebody suddenly makes a statement that seems to come out of the blue. How the group, and especially the group leader, handled that contribution would be crucial. Suppose in the middle of a Bible study, one member said, 'I'm not sure I believe in the resurrection.' Anyone having the security to say that is actually expressing doubt about something that for them is a problem area, and it is not going to be helpful if the leading theologian in the group goes in with nine points to support the evidence for the resurrection. You actually need to explore with that person what their doubts are, before you can respond.

I think a lot then rests with the group leader in giving people space and enabling the rest of the group to hear what is really being said, before any kind of response is made to them.

PJ: It would be a case of responding to the feelings first, responding by saying, 'Tell us more. Let's explore this', rather than letting someone come in with the answers, which might not actually be answering what the real issue is.

PB: That's about pace as well, I think. Are there any other management skills that would prevent conflict in a group?

PJ: A lot of conflict we have been discussing, that gives rise to emotions which then have to be handled, is actually unnecessary and can be avoided. If you are running a committee, for instance, you can make sure that everybody has the minutes, that everybody knows the agenda, everybody is prepared – at least you can do all you can too avoid people feeling lost or left out; that is when they tend to react. So this again depends on the skill of the chairperson in preventing some of the conflict.

PB: That is conflict which is reactionary against something that should have been done properly in the first place and, of course, there is a vast difference between that kind of conflict and the conflict which is creative and explores different sides of an issue. The former is a waste of emotional energy for everybody concerned. I've always felt that the line in the Beatitudes, 'Blessed are the peacemakers', which is often interpreted in the context of somebody coming in and making peace after there has been conflict, applies equally to those who prevent conflict in the first place, by their efficient administration or by the fact that they communicated something very well, or even because people have been trained for particular tasks or roles so that they are functioning in a way that is skilful and helpful to people. My experience in churches is that an awful lot of conflict and unpleasant emotional experiences of anger or threat have actually arisen because something has been communicated very badly or not communicated at all, and people have not known what is happening. I think that it's helpful to look closely at our structures and our systems in churches when it comes to things like administration and communication and the way in which we actually train people.

Emotion can be the forgotten dimension in so many conflict situations. People make changes without considering in advance the feelings likely to be engendered in others; we each expect the other to be rational and reasonable. Most of us in reality have varying degrees of maturity, and therefore of insecurity, so changes do affect us emotionally. Once one person or group acts emotionally that usually threatens the initiator of the change so her reactions are triggered, and so conflicting emotions colour the scene.

REFERENCES

1 David Augsburger, *Caring Enough to Hear and be Heard*, Regal Books, 1982.
2 *Ibid.*
3 Robin Green, *A Step Too Far*, DLT, 1990, p34.
4 For further discussion of this see Harriet Goldhor Lerner's *The Dance of Anger*, Harper & Row, 1989.

CHAPTER 6

CONFLICTING VALUES

'Values' is a word that is frequently used, but which has different shades of meaning. Contained within it is the idea that if a concept and/or practice is important to, or even prized by an individual, it constitutes a value for them, though not necessarily for others.

We are born into cultures, families and societies that impart their values to us. The process continues throughout life, so that values change or develop in the light of new ideas and experiences. There is a developmental dimension to this process in that most young children will unconsciously take on the values of the family. For example, stealing may be seen as wrong or all right. Once in the school culture, children will be exposed to people with other values, and this presents them with the choice of either accepting as their own the assumed values of the family, or of adapting or rejecting that value. This process is accelerated during adolescence when the young person begins to question and explore values originally accepted from others. Decisions are made consciously or unconsciously about which values from the family and culture of birth are intrusive and which are to be affirmed. This process can be hindered by the need for acceptance, so that values can be influenced by the desire to please a particular group or individual such as the peer group, parents or a youth leader.

It is important for those of us who live and work in church cultures to note that relationships which foster dependency promote situations where values, instead of being freely chosen, are imposed. The need for acceptance and to belong can easily, even for adults, encourage the adoption of a particular set of values in order for that individual to maintain a relationship or even to stay in the church. The more emotional investment an individual has in that culture or church, the more power the prevailing cultural values can have over the individual. It is both difficult and painful to put oneself in the position of challenging the prevailing values, especially if such values are being promoted with reference to the Bible or to God's will.

This is particularly pertinent in situations of conflict where strong emotions are being felt. On a recent television programme, someone who had left a church spoke of the trauma of questioning the values of the culture concerning submission to leaders. The experience is more traumatic when individuals want to honour God in their lives and when people for whom they have a profound respect are affirming values that no longer seem to be matching the reality of the individual's situation. The resulting confusion makes it difficult for even mature adults to disentangle themselves and to find out and act upon their own values.

In the first case study, Tom claimed that one of his values was to share his leadership. An inconsistency then arose between his affirmation of this as a value and his actual behaviour. His unilateral decision to remove Colin from the leadership team was inconsistent with his declared commitment to shared leadership.

A story was told recently of a young communist who was interviewed for party membership. He was asked what he would do if he had £100,000. 'That's easy,' was the response. 'I'd give £50,000 to the party.' 'What would you do if you had two houses?' asked the interviewer. Without hesitation the answer came: 'I'd give one to the party and live in the other.' Finally he asked: 'And what if you had two pairs of trousers?' There was a long silence. 'Why the hesitation?' asked the interviewer. 'Because I *have* two pairs of trousers,' replied the young man.

In both the case study and the story it is questionable whether values being claimed were full values. Raths, Harmin and Simon[1] see full values as having these criteria:

CHOOSING   freely
                from alternatives
                after thoughtful consideration of the
                   consequences of each alternative

PRIZING	cherishing, being happy with the choice
	willing to affirm the choice publicly
ACTING	doing something with the choice repeatedly in some pattern of life

Only some of our values are full values. Tom and the young communist in the examples cited above were demonstrating *value indicators*. Some important value indicators are goals, attitudes, beliefs, activities, use of time, use of money and energy, interests and feelings.

It is perfectly possible to hold a certain belief and then discover that it is not freely chosen and therefore it is not really cherished, as Tom found out on the leadership issue. However, in the case of the Harvest committee, Chris demonstrates a very singular approach in his commitment to the Third World elderly: he has been there and worked on a project and is proposing money be invested in similar schemes.

To explore our values is to become more thoroughly aware of ourselves. This could lead us into a process of critical analysis concerning the relationship between our espoused values and our behaviour and actions. It is our belief that the church generally speaking is weak on helping young people and adults to do this. Clarifying values helps people to relate to themselves, to others, to society and to their environment. Whether and how we unify our thoughts, feelings and actions is our own decision as adults, but the church does its members no service in their journey towards maturity if it fails to challenge inconsistency or settles for 'thou shalt' or 'thou shalt not' without real exploration, explanation or opportunity to accept or reject a particular pattern of behaviour. For example, the last thing most parents or youth workers want is for young people to be promiscuous, but young people today will not survive the pressures of their peer culture concerning sexual expression of themselves outside a committed relationship just because they are told by adults that this is sinful. They need a great deal more information, exploration and discussion in order to make a free choice. We may be unhappy or pleased with that choice, but they will exercise self-control only if they have chosen to do so themselves.

Jesus frequently left his listeners with more questions than answers: the challenge was to go on working at the issues.

On the Harvest sub-committee, Peter is willing to ask Sarah and her peers to make a sacrifice in the interests of the poor of the Third World, but from the information we have he does not seem to consider the possibility that financially *he* might be in a better position to do so. Peter's concern for the Third World poor is a value indicator; he wants something to be done, but apparently does not go as far as sacrificing his own lifestyle in the interests of the poor, so his concern is not a full value. Another example might be someone who gets quite angry at the waste of resources when things like glass bottles and newspapers are thrown away. Occasionally he may take such refuse to be recycled; but, more often, because they are cluttering up the garage, the refuse will be dumped into the dustbin. Here the concern is only a value indicator. However, another person will always recycle bottles or paper, and be prepared to organise a collection on behalf of people in the local church. Here the concern and the personal values involved are full values because she is doing everything possible to live by those values.

CLARIFYING VALUES

Find someone you can share this exercise with and take each discussion item one at a time. You will probably need to agree about confidentiality before you begin. (The focus should be on one person at a time.)

Complete each of these unfinished statements in a way that is true for you.

■ What I would really like to tell my church leader is ....
■ What I feel about smoking is ....
■ The reasons for my beliefs about pre-marital/extra-marital sexual relationships are ...
■ As far as the destruction of the rain forests is concerned, I feel ....
■ One value (or behaviour pattern) I would never change is ....

> ■ Something I'm firmly convinced of now but was not X years ago is ....
>
> Help your partner to clarify her response by asking open questions that enable her to explore further her thinking – eg 'Really? Tell me a bit more about your thinking on that?' Avoid closed questions which assume the answer or require only a one word answer – eg 'You don't really think smoking should be banned at work, do you?' 'Do you think that no trees should be felled in Brazil?' Help her to explore her own values and do not disagree or argue whilst the focus is on her. When your turn comes you may hold a different view which your partner will help you to explore.

The issue in question is whether your initial response to the statements above is consistent with your own thought-through values or whether it is a value assumed from your family or culture.

In a church, one of the crucial issues when conflict arises in the decision-making process is whether people would be prepared to apply the same ethical positions to other situations. In other words, if they are saying that they have a value which they want honouring in this particular decision, would they want the same value to be honoured in contexts other than church. For example, Tom believed that Colin and others should submit to his leadership decisions. Does he believe that this is how followers should always respond to leaders? Do Chris and Peter on the Harvest sub-committee believe all money should go only to elderly people in the Third World and never to the elderly in the local community?

It is particularly difficult to separate values from theology in church life. Some of us see our values as coming directly from our theology, and so conflicting values are often about conflicting theologies. On the other hand, we sometimes hold values that have not been exposed to theological consideration, and sometimes what we claim to be a theological belief or value does not become a full value because it fails to influence our behaviour to any noticeable degree. Most Christians claim to be committed to honesty; this is a value derived from their theology. We return to an earlier theme that in most church groups honesty, especially being honest about feelings, rarely manifests itself. It cannot therefore be described as a full value.

In a conflict situation, values are yet another lens through which the whole scenario can be viewed. The values being claimed can be perceived as Christian and be part of the shared cultural values of a community, but while we may all broadly speaking be committed to peace, we may be very divided about donating as a church to CND.

The way we raise or spend money belonging to the church often has people reaching for their values. One person in a church leadership group may believe that the church should not have large savings as this is an inappropriate 'storing up of treasure'. He gives away most of his income, so his value is a full one, and his attitude in church and in his personal life is consistent. Someone else, however, takes the view that God expects us to be good stewards and that it is the responsible way of living life to save something for unforeseen emergencies. She manages her own finances in the light of this value and therefore opposes any suggestion that the church should give away its surplus; here, too, is a full value. Someone else may support the proposal to give away the church surplus and expound the biblical injunction not to store up 'treasure upon earth' whilst continuing to invest personal wealth in the stock market. For this reason, there is inconsistency in this value.

We need to recognise that in all church cultures there are assumed values of greater or lesser importance. These include things like tithing one's income, raising hands and arms in worship songs, belonging to a home group, deferring to a minister, circulating during the Peace, attending communion at least once a week, caring and supporting one another, accepting the decisions of the leadership group – and countless others.

Sometimes people take the assumed values on board unconsciously because they want to be committed, to belong, to be accepted as a member of the community. Later they may modify their thinking and want to ask questions. In some churches this is welcomed (depending on the question), but in others any questioning is discouraged. Where it is discouraged, people are not helped in their journey to maturity. Most families struggle with their adolescents and the church is no different from this. If a person wants to be an adult and make his own decisions about attending a home group, this may be seen as a challenge to the system, and conflict ensues. It is important in churches to give people the space they need to question, to think things through and to make the decisions about what they do and how they do it for themselves. In this way they can build into their own lives behaviour consistent with the values they have freely accepted for themselves.

REFERENCES

1 Raths, Harmin and Simon, *Values and Teaching*, Columbus Ohio, Charles E Merril, 1966, p 28.

CHAPTER 7

CONFLICT SITUATIONS IN THE BIBLE

THE COUNCIL OF JERUSALEM –
ACTS 15

Two conflict situations are described here, one of which ends in apparent consensus and the other which leads to a parting of the ways. The first was of major significance for all of the church as it then existed; the other was rooted more in personal relationships. We want to focus on the conflict that led to the Council of Jerusalem. It is described as a 'sharp dispute and debate' (Acts 15:2). The problem confronting the church in Antioch was that of conflicting theology: some were teaching that circumcision was essential to salvation; Paul and Barnabas disagreed. These two were appointed with others to go to Jerusalem to discuss the issue with the apostles and elders of the church.

It is important to recognise from our knowledge

of people just how much of an emotional issue this would have been. We know from Paul's epistles that he held passionately to a theology of grace; the pressure on the Gentiles to be circumcised would have triggered in him very strong feelings of anger that they were having this yoke put on them. It is not difficult to see how emotional and angry he would have been in challenging those who, from his perception, were harming people he had brought to faith. At the same time, those in the other camp would have been equally passionate in putting their own case, as their security needs were being threatened by Paul's challenge to a long-standing tradition and practice. Here, too, is a conflict of values between those who held firmly and uncompromisingly to a tradition and those who saw the gospel as a challenge to that tradition. Both parties believed they were declaring the will of God; both parties' theology and values were rooted in the word of God, the first in the law and the second in the incarnate Word, Jesus Christ.

Were there conflicting needs? Here we can offer only theories. Those of the circumcision party had a concern to define the boundaries of belonging. This can arise out of a personal insecurity; it is important for some to define who is in and who is out, who belongs and who does not, so that everyone knows the criteria for belonging. It also stems from a need to preserve what is known, tried and tested, and this is sometimes talked of in terms of protecting truth. There are many modern examples of local church and communities where rites of passage such as commitment courses define who belongs.

It is important to note again at this stage that it is perfectly appropriate to draw on theology and to seek to meet needs, but it is more helpful if this can be done in the context of being willing to have one's theology challenged and to explore the needs that are driving us.

Paul and Barnabas certainly had needs: their entire work, over many years, was based on the belief that they lived and preached a gospel of grace. Their whole existence and mission depended on their being free to continue to work as they had always done. If they were wrong, their work was finished; their purpose for living was at stake in this conflict.

One of the most striking aspects of the process of sorting out this conflict is the way in which people were listening to each other. The party of the Pharisees were heard, as were Peter, Paul and Barnabas, and finally James. Peter's contribution is key, not only because of his position in the church but also because he took the argument back to first principles. Here is an excellent example of a leader redefining the problem in terms of the underlying issue. He did not argue about whether Gentiles should obey the whole law of Moses, but pointed back to the fact that, in the purposes of God, separability (ie, apartheid) does not have a place.[1] He argued from experience;[2] James supported this by quoting from the prophets. The argument was lifted from the immediate to the transcendent and this was crucial to the outcome.

The final letter sent to the churches could at face

value be seen as a compromise. Contrasted with the demands for circumcision and a keeping of the whole law of Moses, those made here are very minimal and maybe the focus was on food issues because at the time these were deeply significant for some Jews. We can only speculate, but perhaps the requirements of this letter fitted into their thinking at that time and did not alienate them further until they were able to shift from their Jewish mindset to the Christian one. All that remains in the twentieth century is the expectation that Christians will refrain from sexual immorality, though even here paradigms are shifting in attempts to redefine this in twentieth century culture, for example, with regard to divorce and re-marriage. 'Meat sacrificed to idols' has long since passed into irrelevance.

From what is recorded here in Acts, we can see that there were conflicting values, needs, emotions and theology. There does not seem to have been a conflict over leadership style. The forum for settling the issue seemed to be acceptable to all parties and there seems to have been an expectation that people would be listened and responded to, and that some kind of agreement could be arrived at. Certainly the recognised leaders were a part of the process and, though James set up a proposal, it does not seem that people were looking for him to give authoritarian edicts, but rather to be alongside them in sorting out the issue. This is probably the clearest example of conflict in a group trying to resolve an issue, but some of the same tools can be applied to other incidents.

THE DISTRIBUTION OF FOOD TO WIDOWS – ACTS 6

Here a disagreement arises between the Grecian Jews and the Aramaic-speaking community because their widows were being overlooked in the daily distribution of food. Using the tools outlined in the previous chapters, it is possible to recognise that the Grecian Jews had strong feelings – 'they complained against' – so conflicting emotions were involved. From the reactions of the apostles it seems that this situation had arisen because of their lack of time rather than any wilful neglect of a particular group of widows. The women needed food; the apostles needed to give their time 'to prayer and the ministry of the word'. Here was a conflict of needs. There does not seem to be any conflicting theology or values, at least in so far as there seems to be no disagreement about the need for both distributing food and ministering the word. The proposed solution finds a way of meeting the needs of both groups and therefore of dissipating the conflict.

THE ENTRY INTO THE PROMISED LAND – NUMBERS 13

Moses is trying to make a decision based on information brought back by a group of spies about whether or not to go ahead and move into the promised land. Some of the spies are in favour; others, the majority, are against. The first thing to notice is the different emotions. Caleb and Joshua are confident and hopeful, the others fearful. It could be interpreted that there are different theologies abroad. Joshua (Numbers 14:8) has confidence in the will of God to give them the land. The opposing group make no reference to God and see only the size of the inhabitants. This could have been linked to values: Joshua and Caleb are willing to act on their belief in God's faithfulness; the others are basing their advice on the rational evidence of their own eyes. We need to recognise that there may be some exaggeration around: 'we seemed like grasshoppers in our own eyes, and we looked the same to them.' Needs were different, for Joshua and Caleb represented those who wanted to take risks and move forward, whilst the other group stood for those who were insecure and did not want any more change. This is reinforced by sentiments that expressed a wish to return to Egypt. Their need for security and the emotion of fear are so strong that they talk of choosing another leader and of stoning the opposition. There is real conflict here between leaders and followers, and while Moses obviously supports the view held by Joshua and Caleb, he is unable to persuade the majority.

All these incidents are taking place in contexts and cultures very different from our own; yet it is possible to find here at least some of the factors identified as possibly being present in conflict situations today: needs, theology, styles of leadership/followership, emotions and values.

REFERENCES

1 For a deeper exploration of this issue see Robin Green's
A Step Too Far, DLT, 1990, p55–59.
2 Acts 10.

CHAPTER 8

CHANGE – PREVENTING UNNECESSARY CONFLICT

Introduce change into a church and conflict is inevitable! In conflict situations change is almost always the trigger: someone or a group proposes; someone or a group resists. In the case studies cited earlier, Tom wanted to change the composition of the leadership team; Jim wanted to change the person who was responsible for pouring the tea; the Harvest sub-committee wanted to change where the proceeds from the festival were to go; the vicar wanted to change the interior of the church by adding the Marian statue. These changes caused gigantic waves for some and small ripples for others.

A church is a community, but if it is bigger than a house meeting it is also an organisation. In looking at this, we shall be using a diagram on page 110 adapted from the work of Charles Handy.[1]

Each corner of the triangle represents aspects of the organisation:

■ *People* – recruiting, reassigning, training, learning, support and supervision, counselling.

■ *Systems* – communication, committees, information, budgets, decision-making, reward.

■ *Structures* – services, roles, tasks, groups, buildings.

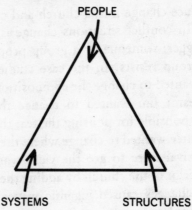

recruiting, reassigning, training
learning, support and supervision
counselling

PEOPLE

SYSTEMS
communication systems
committees
information systems
budgets
decision-making systems
reward systems

STRUCTURES
services
roles
tasks
groups
buildings

It is hard to distinguish between systems and structures. Systems serve a primary function of keeping the organisation running: they are there to 'keep the show on the road'.

The structures – for example, the various groups performing a variety of tasks in different places – are serviced by the systems of providing money, making decisions, conveying information or rewarding by recognising.

One observation that can be made of local churches is that leaders do not usually recognise their churches as organisations. It is therefore quite difficult for those leaders to recognise the effect that change in one part of the organisation can have on another. Handy[2] suggests that the triangle is seen as one side being a steel bar, the second side a piece of string and the third side a rubber band; then it is possible to visualise how changes in one corner will alter the tension in the other two. Removing Colin (the person) affected the role of lay reader and leadership team member (structure) and by-passed the decision-making system vested in a joint leadership team (system). Placing a statue in the church alters the building (structure) about which *people* have opinions and feelings. Do this by ignoring the recognised *systems* for decision-making and conflict is inevitable.

Following Handy, it is important to recognise that the above variables happen within an environment or context. For the local church this includes geographical locality, denomination, wider church,

111

nation and world. In local churches the three most crucial are probably the *goals* or *values*, the *resources* and the *culture*. In some local churches, goals and values are defined, though even if this is the case there can be a mismatch between stated goals and reality. Often goals are vague and assumed rather than articulated. Resources can include people but refers here to equipment and income. Culture refers to beliefs or expectations about the way the church should be organised: for example, how authority is exercised, how people are controlled and/or rewarded, whether people take the initiative or seek permission, what the norm is in dress and practice when attending services, and whether there are rules and procedures or trust and responsibility. The culture will be reinforced in

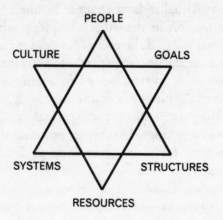

many churches by its 'in' language, songs and heroes (ie, well-known preachers and authors), as well as rituals and customs. Thus the original triangle becomes a star.

It should be realised that in a given context change may sometimes be helpful or sometimes unhelpful.

No change at all	. . . may be death to the organisation.
Too much change, too quickly	. . . may cause unhelpful stress.
Change just for the sake of it	. . . may remove something of value.
HOWEVER Appropriate change	. . . may lead to positive growth and development:

113

(i) if there is stability in one area, whilst changing another;

(ii) if the change is well-thought through and discussed at all levels, perhaps using questionnaires, leaflets and teaching;

(iii) if change is introduced a little at a time.

Sometimes problems arise, not because of the change itself, but because of the way the process of change is handled. Nevertheless, the bigger the change the greater is the adjustment which the people affected have to make. There are occasions when change in churches happens with the speed demonstrated by the car driver who suddenly spots his right turn and takes it without signalling. The driver behind is brought up short and is aware of an alarming rise in heart rate and blood pressure. This driver will experience emotions ranging from mild annoyance to extreme fury. Proper preparation and signalling would have avoided this unnecessary tension. Introducing change in the church needs to be tackled with considered preparation so that people feel as secure as is possible whilst the change is being discussed and implemented.

It needs to be acknowledged that when leaders decide on a change in the church they believe that the change is a part of the purposes of God for that community at that time. This is often expressed as the leading of the Holy Spirit. They are doing what they believe to be right under God. The change may be right but, however much God is involved in it, unless it is introduced with due care and preparation, it will cause disagreement. It is sad if a leader's lack of skill causes conflict, and doubly sad if the ensuing disharmony is blamed on members of the congregation for being resistant to the Holy Spirit and to God's leading. People may be resistant for a variety of reasons, but spiritualising resistance in this way can be a means of scapegoating others for the inadequate management of change on the part of the leadership. This is not to deny that some people will resist change at all costs, but it serves to emphasise that leaders need to do all in their power to ensure that conflict and stress do not enter the situation through their lack of skill.

If we focus on the 'people' point of the star diagram, we can explore some of the reasons why change causes conflict. Colin and Ada were removed from a role without being consulted. For both of them there was a shock element. They had previously felt valued in the fulfilment of that role, but they were removed, made redundant and told, for different reasons, that they were inadequate. In fact, their contribution to their community was rejected and devalued, and they felt devalued as persons. Those witnessing these scenarios, who were in any way sensitive to Ada or Colin, felt angry at the injustice as they perceived it. The changes, for whatever reason they were made, were not skilfully implemented.

We do not know whether the Harvest committee made changes or not, but it is not hard to imagine the feelings that will be aroused in the church and village if the money is given to the Third World instead of the local people. Those who gave generously, thinking it was for local folk, will react; those who lose by not being in receipt of a Christmas hamper will feel the loss, not only materially but also in the symbolism of the care and concern of their neighbours.

The vicar who placed a statue in the church building after being refused a faculty flouted democratic procedures, a practice calculated to spark conflict in most contexts. Given that such a change will impinge on theological concerns and threaten values, one might be tempted to ask whether this is just ineptness or deliberate confrontation which will lead to a walk out by those who feel most strongly.

MANAGING CHANGE

Managing change is primarily to do with helping people to handle change and not just about getting a task done. Often the individual or group wanting to implement change sees it as obvious progress or an improvement on the existing arrangement. This will never be everybody's perception. Proposed changes in churches often spring from one individual's or one group's values, and within the one-church community values will differ between groups and individuals.

Because of this, anyone wanting to propose change in any form would be wise to bear in mind that success is not guaranteed. Sometimes the opposition is so great that more harm would be done to the community by insisting on the change than by not implementing it. Also, when all aspects of the change are considered and aired in an atmosphere of mutual co-operation, the change may become unnecessary, or the proposer may have second thoughts. If change comes about through democratic process and people are valued throughout, any one of these results is possible. There is a strong link here with the ideas on leadership and followership styles discussed in Chapter four. Authoritarian leaders and deferential followers will have problems working with the model outlined in this chapter.

If, then, you were thinking about proposing a change, it would be helpful to talk it through with one or two people with whom you have a secure relationship, inviting them to ask difficult questions and to push you to explore your reasons and motivations for wanting this change. If, after that, you still feel it is right for you to go ahead, you will need to identify two groups of people in the church:

(i) those who will be most affected by the change
(ii) those who are most respected and listened to

The first group, since they are the ones who have the most to lose and possibly the most to gain, will obviously need your special attention and consideration; the second group are the ones in the community who are the leaders of thought (though not necessarily the actual leaders), and if you cannot convince them of the value of your idea you are unlikely to carry the rest of the church. In talking to these two groups you should remember that real communication is as much about listening and responding as it is about talking and telling.

This process needs to be done in such a way as to gain people's support and not in a way that threatens either them or things that are important to them. It may also be worth considering the possibility that church life is for many people what Alvin Toffler[3] called a 'stability zone'. He suggests that people living with a lot of change and stress in their lives need stability zones in order to conserve energy and manage stress.

The work place for many in industry, the education service, the health service and local government has been the scene of unremitting change in recent years and it would not be surprising if those living with high levels of stress at work were to look to their church as a stability zone. Any proposed change there would be threatening and therefore to be resisted. Awareness of the environment is very important. At the same time, a church which cannot adapt to changing circumstances, which is unable to grow and develop, will stagnate and cease to meet the needs of those both within and without. In fact, it is important that the church is a stability zone, but it should be possible to have stability in some areas of church life whilst making changes in others.

When talking with those you perceive as being respected leaders of thought, and some of these may also fall into the category of being affected by the change, it is vital to create an awareness of the need for change, preferably by demonstrating to them objective facts in the situation.

Always be open to allowing people to contribute suggestions and counter-suggestions so that, by investing their ideas in the proposed change, they increasingly own it. Deal gently with those who are resistant. Rather than demolishing their argument, try to discern what their real difficulty is and give attention to that. Often people are resistant because, at heart, they are afraid of the change. It is that fear that needs exploring and addressing, not necessarily the apparent argument the other person is putting forward.

Advancing more and more arguments can put people so much on the defensive that they become entrenched in their positions and perhaps isolated. This is when conflict can become damaging to individuals and to the community; people start to polarise and take sides. It takes time and patience, the hallmarks of enabling leaders. Those with a more authoritarian style will find this process very difficult to work with.

If unhelpful conflict is to be minimised at a time of change, the 'systems' part of the star diagram will be very significant. Effectiveness of communication in any organisation is often the test of organisational health. In addition, people will need preparation and

119

training for any change of role they are being asked to undertake. Peacemaking is as much about preventing strife as it is about restoring peace after conflict. 'Blessed are the peacemakers', the effective commuicators, those who take training seriously. Subsequent chapters explore ways of communicating which may be appropriate at different times and in different situations, and also ways in which, through training, people can be prepared for new responsibilities.

REFERENCES

1 Charles B Handy, *Understanding Organisations*,
Penguin Business Publictions, 3rd edition, 1985, p 369.
2 *Ibid*.
3 Toffler A, *Future Shock*, Bodley Head, 1970.

CHAPTER 9

COMMUNICATION – PREVENTING UNNECESSARY CONFLICT

In our experience of local churches, the common method of communication is 'the grapevine'. If the appropriate people fail to communicate, someone else will, because people usually find a way of getting answers to their questions or information about what is going on. The grapevine is speedy but rarely wholly accurate. Grapevine information may be distorted and exaggerated, often omitting significant information. It is difficult to stop the flow once started for it has a high degree of credibility. If tension and unnecessary conflict is to be avoided, the leadership needs a system of communication which, like the grapevine, reaches all parts of the church.

A leadership team will need to work out guidelines for everyone on what is being communicated, who is to do the communicating and, immensely important, *how* it is to be done. In many churches, communication is often inconsistent and patchy because there is neither a communication policy nor a system. Consequently the whole process is erratic.

We should like to suggest that a local church needs to communicate the following information:

- Names and information about those who hold significant roles, eg leaders, administrator, organist, group leaders.
- Changes in personnel such as changes in responsibility: those stepping down and those taking on a role.
- The structures and the thinking behind them.
- The history and development of the church.
- Vision and goals of the church.
- Current and proposed changes.
- Financial situation.
- Relations with other churches and with the local community.
- Views on current issues such as pollution and conservation.
- Any specific policies.

This is not an exhaustive list, but a willingness to share news and information openly carries a message to church members about their importance within the community; it is saying, 'Because this information concerns the church, it also concerns you.'

Look at the above list and tick any information *your* church consistently communicates to its members. Add anything else you may think of but which is not on the list.

HOW CAN THE INFORMATION BE COMMUNICATED?

One-way: downwards

whole church meeting
notices in church
posters
church magazine
written bulletin in pews
annual report
personal letters
exhibitions

Two-way: upwards/downwards

briefing groups
committees/councils
one-to-one
open invitation meetings
home groups
induction programmes

One-way: upwards

suggestion box
response to questionnaires
absenteeism, lateness, walkouts

Any direction

church magazine
telephone
memos
reports
grapevine

> In your perception, which methods have been
> used helpfully or unhelpfully in your church?
>
> By which of these methods do you *prefer*
> to receive information? Which do you like the
> *least*?
>
> What are the advantages and disadvantages
> of each method for (a) leaders in the church,
> (b) church members.

Whatever your response to the above questions, we
want to emphasise that the fundamental communication skill is that of listening. This is vital for all of
us. Many problems arise because we misinterpret
what others – leaders or congregation – are actually
saying.

> **Read the following questions and try to
> respond with an honest yes or no**
>
> ■ Do you give full attention to a speaker by
> looking at them as well as by listening to
> them?
> ■ Do you try to follow their reasoning
> carefully?
> ■ Do you listen for the feelings underlying the
> words?
> ■ Do you keep listening even when you hear
> something you think is wrong (or you disagree
> with)?
> ■ Do you allow for your own bias and feelings
> as you weigh the arguments?
> ■ Do you really consider the other person's

point of view before you respond?
■ Are you willing for the other to have the last word?

In some of the case studies, communication was not particularly skilful. Tom almost ceased communicating at all by withdrawing. His approach to Colin was very much 'downwards' even when he saw him in person. Jim also distanced himself from Ada, but then Ada did not seek out Jim either. The Harvest sub-committee were working at resolution and so have every chance of avoiding disaster if they keep listening and responding. The vicar and the statue is an example of one-way communication, the imposing of a decision to have the statue, and it resulted in a walk-out by at least one member of the church.

Skilful listening helps a speaker to feel valued because he feels he is being heard. The listener also gains in that there is often an improved relationship arising from a better understanding of the other. In addition, the listener is in possession of accurate information about the thinking, the opinions and the feelings of the speaker, which could lead to a creative resolution of any difficulties.

CHAPTER 10

TRAINING PEOPLE – PREVENTING UNNECESSARY CONFLICT

In local churches, people are invited to take on all kinds of roles and jobs, often carrying considerable responsibility but without offering any kind of contract, job description, review procedure, training, support or supervision. There is a growing trend for lay people to have greater involvement in the church's ministry so that tasks are shared.

These people are volunteers. In society at large, volunteers are increasingly having a role to play in community-based projects such as with counselling agencies and in charity shops. Very many of these undergo training for the new role to prevent problems arising and to ensure that they have the skills to do the job for which they have volunteered. Apart from the need to have the job done well, this approach values the person, making him more likely to succeed and to feel good about doing the job.

Yet it is quite usual in local churches for people to be expected to lead a small group, without necessarily having any knowledge of how groups work. Pastoral visiting is another area in which the laity assist the minister. Often these visits will involve people or families who are going through a time of stress and any visitor will need, at the very least, good listening skills and possibly counselling skills if she is to avoid doing real damage to the situation. There are also committees to chair, and we can all recall meetings which were anything from completely ineffective to downright damaging to the organisation, owing to the poor skills of the chairperson. Churches expect people to be able and willing to perform all these tasks, and it is only the fortunate few who are able to bring skills from another sphere such as their professional lives.

Conflict can occur in churches when people are appointed and then seem to perform the task inadequately. In many churches a particular job has no job description, and a person's failure to fulfil the role may be because some part of it was not even known – 'I didn't know I was supposed to . . .' is a familiar refrain. It should not be forgotten that such failures, as well as being damaging to the church, are deeply upsetting for the individual and may affect self-concept and self-esteem to such a degree that withdrawal takes place.

In the church, because people want to be seen as a community, family or fellowship, there is sometimes a reluctance to make use of job descriptions and contracts. It is a sad reflection on an organisation when it fails to value its volunteers by not communicating to them clearly what is involved in the job, what both sides expect, and the level of support and supervision on offer to ensure growth and development. If someone is being invited to take on the role of, for example, home group leader, it is necessary to know whether his expectations match those of either the group or the church leadership. Where there is a mismatch in expectations there is the potential for conflict.

A job description and a contract are valuable tools for leaders in making clear what is involved; the new volunteer would be helped by being assured of the necessary support and training as the job description is discussed.

Training for service is an integral part of being a Christian disciple. Failure to integrate training into the local church agenda means that people do not see training as a part of their discipleship. Some churches put a strong emphasis on people developing their relationship with God, with the expectation that they will grow in this aspect of their lives. Little emphasis is given to the need for growth and development in ministry and service. This is when helpers, though willing at first, can become disillusioned, and if they opt out this can lead to conflict, as can any criticism of their mistakes either by leaders or by church members. Such mistakes might have been avoided through training.

It is not possible to explore every area, but at this
point it would be appropriate to focus on just one
function that many people are called upon to undertake, that of chairing a small group. These come in
many guises – for Bible study, prayer, decision-
making or even to perform a particular task. It is in
such small groups that a great deal of conflict arises
and it can be handled constructively or destructively.
In our experience, very few chairpersons have any
real understanding of how groups work.

One way of looking at any working group is to
see that it is composed of three elements:

■ individuals
■ the task
■ the needs that maintain the group

Though each of these elements has its own needs,
significant areas will be held in common.

Every group comes into being for a purpose. Its
task may be either specific or broad, may remain the
same or be changed, may be well or ill-defined. If it
has no task it has no reason to exist. It is interesting

that in current industrial management parlance there is a need for any organisation to have a 'mission statement'. Conflict may arise if the task is ill-defined, or if it is re-defined without discussion, creating confusion amongst members. It would be fascinating to know the process by which the Wimbledon Croquet Club became the world famous Tennis Club!

Take a few minutes to recall and list all the groups in your church, and to define them according to their tasks or purposes.

The group also needs to experience success. Without this there is decreasing motivation. We know of a Residents' Association whose meetings are constantly postponed for lack of interest because the purpose for which it was called into being has met with very little success. It, like all groups, needs a strategy in order to fulfil its task, one which will lead to some degree of success if the group is to continue.

The circle in the diagram concerned with individual needs acknowledges that every person brings some needs to a task-related group. Probably the strongest one is to belong and feel accepted. In addition, most people have a need to contribute, to be valued and to be recognised. If these needs are not met, some may not continue in the group, but even if they do, because they feel little or no acceptance, they will often be unable to express disagreement or feelings during a discussion. If they do not feel valued, they will not feel listened to, so why should they speak?

Group maintenance needs have to be met if the group is to function effectively. This includes clear lines of communication, mutual respect and support, a common desire for effective teamwork and a need continually to improve the level of understanding. In the diagram the circles are interlocked and in counter-tension; failure or malfunction in one area affects the other two. A person who does not feel accepted and who responds to that with an emotional reaction can prevent himself and others from concentrating on the task. A feeling of not getting anywhere in the task

132

affects motivation and can lessen the individual's desire to belong or to support the team effort.

In a group responsible for leading a church or part of a church's ministry, group maintenance needs have to be met if differences of opinion are to be handled constructively and creatively. This can be done only if everyone has a sufficient sense of acceptance to be able to express opinions and feelings openly. If this freedom is lacking then a variety of different things can happen. Some people may withdraw emotionally or even physically; some may become manipulative, consciously or unconsciously; others may use their authority of position or expertise in order to coerce; yet others may become resistant or unco-operative. A power struggle for influence thus emerges.

Having some understanding of groups may be helpful to a chairperson, but even more helpful would be some skills training. Group maintenance needs are not usually met by chance. It takes some skill to build in a group or committee an environment of trust where people feel they know each other well enough to give expression, to listen and to respond to honest opinions and feelings. It is skilful chairing that helps a group to support the risks that people take. For example, a quiet person risks speaking for the first time; someone risks a minority opinion; someone else makes herself vulnerable by admitting some fear or other emotion.

If differences and emotions do not surface, it is possible that an issue will not be explored properly.

If such feelings and differences are actually suppressed, they can fester and erupt either in another context or in the same group at a later meeting. Genuine communication can mean that there is some rawness in the group, but where differences and emotions can be acknowledged and worked through, any ultimate decision will be more likely to be owned and supported.

Handling emotions such as anger in a group, particularly if people are confronting one another, requires quite a high level of skill, but conflict handled openly and honestly is usually more constructive than suppressed conflict which can be exceedingly destructive not only in the specific group but also in the church. This is the challenge for Keith as he chairs the Harvest committee through its next phase and on to a decision.

For you to consider

Reflect on the groups and committees in which you are or have been involved. Assess the level of honest communication and your own skill, whatever your role, in handling differences of opinion and expressions of feeling. Is training needed? If so, in what areas?

Chairing or leading a small group is only one example of a task many are asked to take on with insufficient preparation and training. Many churches appoint children's workers who are young both in years and experience yet who are expected to work with very little training with a group of young children. This creates a potential for damage to children and conflict with parents; some children will opt out if the experience is negative, with God and the church forever being associated with that experience. The same would be true with youth work, and young people do not tolerate lack of skill in their leaders. Whatever the task, if in our churches we want to avoid stress and conflict for those involved in doing the task and those at the receiving end, we need to take preparation and training seriously.

CHAPTER 11

MEDIATION – FOR CASES OF DEADLOCK

There are occasions in church life when persons or groups become so estranged or alienated that the parties themselves are unable to relate in any constructive dialogue. Apart from the Society of Friends, few denominations seem to have taken the concept of mediation seriously. This is surprising because, although the term itself occurs infrequently in the Bible, the idea of mediation permeates throughout. The term 'mediator' belongs pre-eminently to Christ, the 'one mediator between God and men' (1 Timothy 2:5). The function of a mediator is to intervene between the two parties in order to promote the relationship between them when the parties themselves seem unable to do so. The mediator aims to effect conciliation or reconciliation. Joab took on the role of mediator between David and Absalom (2 Samuel 14:1–23), and the prophet and priestly roles were mediatory – the former mediating as God's spokesman, the latter acting on behalf of humanity in the presence of God.

It may be that mediation is so little used because we in the church actually have problems recognising and acknowledging that a conflict can reach such a state of impasse that relations are broken off. We want to deny that this could happen. There are people within larger denominational groupings, such as dioceses and regions, who have special responsibilities for activities such as adult education, counselling and exorcism. However, denominations do not, to our knowledge, train or make available skilled mediators whom local churches could use in the same way that industry might call on ACAS (Advisory, Conciliation and Arbitration Service) to help in the resolution of an industrial dispute.

It is extremely difficult for an individual to act as a mediator in the same church to which she belongs where an issue has caused a serious breakdown of relationships. At the same time, there may be occasions when this *is* possible if that individual is not involved in the conflict and can be seen by all as detached from it. The key, if a third party is to be effective, is that he must be seen by both parties to be neutral and unbiased. If people are to communicate honestly and openly, as they must if they are to move towards resolution, they need to feel some degree of safety. If one party is anxious that the mediator might side with the other party, feelings of safety are eroded. Both sides need to be able to trust the person and the skill of the mediator. This applies whether it is a situation of deadlock between two home group members or between two warring committees.

Resolution will begin only when the parties communicate directly with one another about their conflict. Neither side will be ready to attempt reconciliation until the considerable flow of angry energy towards the other has been expressed. The frustration which causes the anger arises because each party sees the other as a blocking factor in achieving certain objectives. This leads to the 'fight or flight' mechanism coming into play, when the human response, in a situation that is sensed as dangerous, is to be aggressive (fight) or to retreat (flight). People rarely fight with fists in the church, but angry words can be used to demolish an opponent. Perhaps more common is flight or withdrawal. Sometimes this is physical; at other times it is emotional and takes the form of distancing. As long as the parties involved avoid each other, resolution is virtually impossible, though both types of withdrawal are a means of self-protection.

Whether the situation is large scale or small scale, mediation offers both sides a procedure which:

- values their emotions
- provides an active listener or audience through the mediator
- brings the parties together in a safe place
- empowers people so that they can choose how much or little to say
- explores perceptions in order to focus the issues

- restores proportion and perspective
- builds on common ground
- uses a process so that people can defend their interests without overwhelming the other party.

A *mediator* therefore needs considerable maturity and skill. We have already suggested that she needs to be neutral. In addition to this, the mediator must avoid having any investment in the outcome of the procedure. A mediator is not there to find a solution but to enable the parties to do so. At the same time if the mediator has an emotional need to achieve 'success', she is investing too much in the process and will not be able to maintain the necessary detachment. If the parties agree to disagree then a mediator as well as the parties concerned need to see this as a valid conclusion to the mediation process.

The skills of a mediator lie in his capacity to work with people to build trust. He needs also to be able to defuse anger and to listen actively, communicating empathy to both parties. Crucial to the role is the need to help those involved to express themselves clearly. When they feel strongly about something, people can often confuse perception, fact, prejudice, assumption, opinion and, last but not least, emotion. In a conflict scenario, these factors can be even more confused than usual. Somehow a mediator has to help the parties disentangle these strands in order to focus on the things which are relevant. Finally, a mediator needs to be able to think creatively in order to ask the kind of questions which enable people to think creatively themselves when a stage is reached where some kind of resolution seems possible.

> Before reading on, imagine that you have been asked to mediate in Tom's church between Tom and Colin. Jot down an order of procedure and also what, in general terms, you hope might be achieved at each stage.
>
> Alternatively, think of a situation known to you where two individuals had a breakdown of relationship. Jot down an order of procedure and also what you hope might be achieved at each stage.

MEDIATING IN ACTION

1 The initial task of the mediator is to set up some kind of contract or agreement with the parties which makes clear to everyone what is expected of each. It is essential that any resolution is strictly the preserve of the parties and that the outcome of the mediation procedure may be to agree to differ. It is not the task of the mediator to find a resolution and certainly not to impose one. Other things that might be in an initial contract include relating to each other with respect, a commitment to listen without interrupting, an openness to looking for creative ways out of the deadlock. It may not be possible to get the parties to negotiate

an agreement but at least the mediator should make clear his own role and expectations and ask the parties if they are willing to accept these.

2 The mediation procedure could involve meeting with the parties together from the outset, but some mediators prefer initially to meet separately with the parties to allow each to express their perception of the conflict in relative safety, free from possible counter argument. This procedure can help to engender trust in the mediator.

3 When finally everyone gets together, at least one full hour will be necessary with an agreed time for closing. It is best not to exceed two hours. The session needs to be free from interruption and on neutral ground. Everyone should be able to see the others comfortably, with the mediator seated in a central position. In a Christian setting, it may be appropriate to suggest that participants be quiet for a moment and think over prayerfully the reasons for the meeting. The mediator may wish to bring those few moments to a conclusion by using a brief one-line prayer such as 'May the Lord be with us', inviting a brief response from the participants.

4 Both sides should be asked to prepare opening statements that focus primarily on feelings, but could include any background to how the problem arose. Essential is how it feels and why it feels as it does, followed by what the person would like to happen now. The focus is feelings and not demands because

feelings encourage sympathy and understanding, whilst demands encourage defensiveness and entrenching in solid positions.

5 Encouraging constructive communication requires a high level of skill; some of the ways to help people separate fact from prejudice as they share their views have been outlined above. Essential to the process is the need to try to prevent either side from disengaging and to support any conciliatory gestures. Clarification skills are essential: 'Are you saying that ...?', or 'That sounds as if you felt ...' In addition, the skill of immediacy is extremely important; for instance, it may be necessary to say, 'I have a feeling we have got a bit stuck. Is that how you feel? What do we do about it?'

6 At some point of the process, the mediator needs to judge the time to intervene with a question that focuses the dialogue on what the participants really want in order to establish their real needs and interests. This is a process of moving people from the positions they have adopted to an examination of the needs behind the interests. In addition, some very gentle confrontation may be necessary to help individuals to focus on the issues behind what they are saying. Remember that conflict is about conflicting needs, emotions, values, and theology. A search for creative ways forward might be achieved through brainstorming, playing devil's advocate, or even redefining the confronting problem. Respect for those

taking part must underpin the use of all these skills.

7 If some kind of agreement is arrived at, it is helpful if this can be put into writing. One way of doing this is for the mediator to write out the first draft and then invite criticisms from everyone until all are agreed that what is written is an accurate summary of the agreement reached as a conclusion to the mediation process.

The above is a bare outline of a mediation process and it would be advisable for anyone thinking of undertaking such a role to read further and if possible to seek training. Given the amount of conflict in local churches, it would be good to see individuals ready to work within their own churches where the problem is fairly contained, perhaps between two people, but also to see a development of a ministry of mediation in the various denominational structures.

CHAPTER 12

CONCLUSION

It has already been suggested that the major catalyst of conflict in any organisation is that of *change*. If we can manage change, we may be able to manage conflict constructively. Conflict is constructive when authentic communication takes place around the issues which arise and where this leads to the persons concerned engaging with real problems and getting involved in solving them. The result of this kind of activity can be a greater group cohesiveness, personal growth and lastly, but just as important as these, the release of suppressed feelings of fear, energy or stress.

Destructive conflict drains energy away from individuals and often from more important activities. It is unhelpful when it widens the gulf between individuals or groups by exaggerating differences in values, which results in polarisation and defensive, hardened attitudes and positions. All this can prove very stressful, often destroying morale and negatively influencing people's self-concept.

Change is often proposed by those in leadership,

but this is not always the case. Sometimes it is a recognised leader who is seeking to impose change on a church, but there are times when a particular group wants to impose change on everyone else. This can happen particularly over style of worship.

If we recognise a conflict situation arising which we want to try to turn into a constructive rather than a destructive one, it may be helpful to start by identifying clearly the catalyst. Who is wanting to change what, and why? This is where the tools explored in Chapters two to seven may be of practical value for looking at the needs, values, theology, leadership/followership styles involved; and the emotions that are surfacing. The same tools need to be used for looking at those resisting the change. If, for example, we identify a clash of needs, the possible positive outcome is that people start exploring ways of meeting everyone's needs and take up a common problem-solving approach. If, however, the individuals or group concerned believe they have had a word from God, they may be intractable.

If seeking to initiate change, however minimal we might feel it is, a prerequisite might be to sit down and list all the people who will be affected by the proposed change, in what ways they will be affected and how they will feel about those changes. This exercise might make us reconsider our aims. However, if we decide to proceed, we need to plan a considered strategy which aims to involve other people and to carry them with us. This will require patience and tolerance but may achieve change without too many casualties. To impose change suddenly, assuming we have the power to do so by virtue of role or sheer numbers, can achieve what we want but at a very high cost to some of the individuals or groups who for whatever reason (sometimes it may be a sound reason) get in the way. Tools for this process include effective communication and training.[1]

Conflict can begin to appear within a small group like a home group when no apparent change has been suggested or initiated by the leader. Usually this is because one or more members of the group is in some way unhappy or dissatisfied with the present way of doing things. It needs to be recognised that this is someone wanting something done differently; the person may not be very specific but he would like something changed. It is surprising how adults can tolerate something, which in some cases could be amicably renegotiated, at the same time as communicating non-verbally (or at least not openly) their dissatisfaction. In this situation it may be helpful for the leader who recognises this is happening to see the individual concerned on his own and, by using the tools outlined in Chapters two to seven, to try to pinpoint what the problem is. It could be an older person who feels that the group finishes too late: their need is to be home by 10 pm. Once this need is identified, the whole group could then explore ways of changing its timings in order to meet the need. It would be important to take it to the whole group because, if the leader decided to make a change unilat-

147

erally with only the support of the person who proposed the change, the outcome could be a negative reaction from other group members who find an earlier starting time difficult. The leader needs to bring the older person's point of view to the whole group as a problem to share so that the issue is resolved with everyone's co-operation and involvement.

More delicate might be a clash of style in a home group: a leader may incline towards being authoritarian and a group member finds this difficult; or the style of the leader is to enable wide-ranging discussion involving everybody, and a group member would prefer straight input. It should be appreciated that this also is a desire for change. If it emerges as a result of individual discussion that a clash of style is the problem, it may be possible to support the person into accepting the style by explanation, or even for the leader to adjust her style on occasions to accommodate that individual's needs. Another alternative might be for the person concerned to move to another group where the leadership style is more in keeping with his expectations. If conflict becomes so debilitating that there is a breakdown in communication and relationships, mediation may be necessary to redeem the whole situation.

Creative conflict is always to be welcomed. It is through diverse and different opinions, perceptions, understandings and ideas being brought to bear on an issue pertinent to the life of a group or an organisation like the local church that growth and development can be corporately experienced.

To achieve this, there needs to be a certain amount of self-awareness that enables us to recognise our own motives, needs and values, as well as to help others recognise and give expression to theirs. Armed with this knowledge, we may be able to offer leadership in a change process as real peace *makers* because we will be equipped to relate to others with integrity, honesty and vulnerability so that ensuing dialogue is real and constructive for as many people as possible. This is applicable whether the initiative is coming from the leader or from a member of the group or congregation, and whether we are leading a small home group or a congregation of several hundred.

REFERENCES

1 For an exploration of liturgical changes, see Trevor Lloyd's *Introducing Liturgical Change*, Grove Worship Series No 87. The principles outlined could apply to any denomination.

USING THIS BOOK IN GROUPS OR COMMITTEES

All the exercises and activities in this book could be used by groups. They will work best if people work first in sub-groups of twos, threes or fours to do the initial activity and sharing. Larger groups can intimidate and inhibit discussion. The sub-groups then feed back *significant* points from their work together to the whole group.

As a conclusion to the activity, the chairperson or group leader should allow sufficient time for the group to address two questions:

(i) What do we learn as a group from this activity?

(ii) Do we need to change the way we do things and if so how?

The usefulness of spending time in this way will depend on how well this group can carry through the 'how' question.

It may be helpful for someone to share something of the context of the chapter by either reading or summarising the relevant parts, before or after the exercise. The group leader will need to decide when this is appropriate; for example, the exercise in the middle of Chapter one, 'What is your view?' depends on the group's having read the case study, whereas the exercise at the beginning of Chapter three, 'How do you see God?' is best tackled without reference to the contents of that chapter. In the discussion following the exercise, some of the chapter content could be referred to and shared with the whole group.

Chapter eight may be particularly useful to those groups making changes in their own grouping, or changing things for others in their church. If this is the case, instead of doing the suggested exercise about changes to a church service, they could take their own proposed change and explore its implications using the suggested questions. The shared findings and thinking could then be used to decide:

(i)   whether the change should go ahead
(ii) if so, how to handle it with skill and sensitivity by anticipating some of the tension points
(iii) what questions need to be asked, such as who is going to do what, how, and when?

The key to useful group work on any of these issues is to take an exercise and adapt it to the needs of the group at that particular time.

FURTHER READING

Groups and Committees

The Red Book of Groups and How to Lead them Better, Gail Houston, The Rochester Foundation, 1984.

Growing Christians in Small Groups, John Mallinson, Scripture Union, 1989.

Once Upon A Group, Michael Kindred, pub Michael Kindred, 20 Dover Street, Southwell, Notts NG25 0EZ.

Joining Together, D Johnson & F Johnson, Prentice Hall, 3rd Edition, 1987.

Decision Making

Lateral Thinking, Edward de Bono, Penguin, 1977.

Group Decision Making, Ed. W C Swap, Sage, 1984.

Lifeskills Now: Creative Decision Making and *Lifeskills Now: Problem Solving*, B Hopson & M Scally, 1989.

Values

A Practical Guide to Value Clarification, M Smith, University Associates, 1977.

Change

Managing change and making it stick, R Plant, Gower, 1987.

Change: The Challenge for Management, V Stewart, McGraw Hill, 1983.

Introducing Liturgical Change, Trevor Lloyd, Grove Worship Series No 87, 1984.

Conflict

Learning from Conflict, Lois B Hart, Addison Wesley, 1981.

Conflicts – a better way to resolve them, Edward de Bono, Harrap, 1985.

Training

Grow Your Own Leaders, A Baumohl, Scripture Union, 1987.

Emotions

Working up a storm: anger, anxiety, joy, tears on the job and how to handle them, J M Plass & K V Hoover Dempsey, Norton, 1988.

Mediation

Everyone can win: How to resolve conflict, Helena Cornelius and Shoshana Faive, Simon and Schuster, 1989.

TRAINING AGENCIES

The following agencies offering courses in skills areas outlined in this book:

Administry, 69 Sandridge Road, St Albans, Herts. AL1 4AG – courses, papers and resources relating to church administration and organisation.

The Training Unit, Scripture Union, 26–30 Heathcoat Street, Nottingham NG1 3AA – courses and resources for small group work, management of organisations, conflict and communication, committees and teams.

Group Relations Training Association, 12 Fabian Road, London SW6.

Surrey University, Department of Educational Studies, University of Surrey, Guildford GU2 5XH – group facilitator skills.

National Council For Voluntary Organisations, 26 Bedford Square, London WC13 3HU – courses on small group leadership, committees, etc.

Kingston Friends Workshop Group, 78 Eden Street, Kingston upon Thames, Surrey KT1 1DJ – mediation and conflict management.

Australia and New Zealand

Contact: The Conflict Resolution Network, P O
Box 1016, Chatswood, NSW 2057, Telephone (02) 419 8500, Fax (02) 4131148.

They can supply contacts for all States and
Territories in Australia, and for New Zealand.